Hi Patti,

This book will
resonate with
you as it's all
about creating
a system that
enables learning
and development.

Sincerely,

D...l...di...

6.7.21

# SACRED WORKDAY

## How to Create an Awe-Inspiring Business

DANIEL CUSTÓDIO

Printed in the United States of America

First Printing, 2018

Cover photo by Freddie Marriage (freddiemarriage.com)

ISBN:  1986676803
ISBN-13:  978-1986676809

For my wife and three daughters

This book took away sacred time from us and I wouldn't have been able to complete it without your support.

# CONTENTS

# FOREWORD

On the first day of my course in Lean, I tell my students at the University of Massachusetts that the world is still less than ten percent of the way through its Lean journey. Their parents' generation has had real trouble implementing Lean and has left them an enormous opportunity. I let them know that they should be excited as they head out into a business world that has yet to embrace this powerful new paradigm.

In his book *The Structure of Scientific Revolutions*, T.S. Kuhn wrote about how difficult it was for people to switch paradigms. Throughout history, people have had trouble when a dramatically different explanation comes along for how some aspect of the world works. It can take a lot to get them to accept the new paradigm, no matter how superior it is to the old one.

Lean is a complete game changer. It leads to levels of performance that are literally impossible under "traditional" management approaches. And yet, truly Lean organizations are still scarce, as are leaders who truly embrace Lean. In addition to all the things T.S. Kuhn wrote about how people are blind to new paradigms, Lean has an additional and significant strike against it – it requires a complete change in behavior from leaders and managers. And it isn't something they can delegate, even a little bit.

On the cognitive side, Lean is very counterintuitive at first. It requires a completely different mindset from traditional management. Almost everything changes. What was important before, is no longer important, and vice-versa. Lean takes considerable time to learn and internalize. This is why one of the first pieces of advice given to people wanting to implement Lean is to get a good teacher or sensei.

Daniel Custodio is a true Lean sensei. Not only is he an experienced Lean practitioner, but he is a clear thinker, and has a thoughtful and fresh perspective on how to explain Lean. As well as providing a good sense of the underlying philosophy (without which you won't get very far), this book is full of tips, tactics, and interesting nuggets of wisdom. It is just as you would expect from both someone who is both a doer and a thinker. You are in very good hands here.

Taiichi Ohno, the architect of Lean at Toyota, used to say that the Toyota Production System was the logical extension of what Henry Ford did at River Rouge. And as I read this book, I couldn't help but be reminded of what Henry Ford used to say, *Thinking is hard – which is why so few people do it.*

Lean dramatically raises the bar for the rigor of thinking required from people at all levels in an organization. This does indeed make it hard work, but it is more than worth the effort.

I hope you enjoy this book.

Alan Robinson
Co-author of *Ideas Are Free* and *The Idea-Driven Organization*
Professor, Isenberg School of Management, UMass

# NOTE FROM THE AUTHOR

A *torii* is a traditional Japanese gate that marks the entrance to a sacred space. On the cover of this book is the Fushimi Inari Shrine, which has 10,000 torii leading up to its doors. I put that image there because the contents inside of this book are sacred to me and I hope that one day they will also become sacred to you.

But what is sacred?

Brett and Kate McKay offer a thought-provoking analysis on the matter in their article entitled, *The Power of Ritual: The Creation of Sacred Time and Space in a Profane World*. In the article, they quote Mircea Eliade, a leading interpreter of religious experience, who established paradigms in religious studies. According to Eliade, there are two modes of being: sacred and profane. The former represents *fascinating and awe-inspiring mystery — a "manifestation of a wholly different order" from our natural (or profane) everyday lives.*[1] The latter represents the rut most people are stuck in as part of their day-to-day routine that leads to restlessness, apathy, alienation, and general boredom.

In the article, they go onto mention the importance of rituals as the vehicle that transforms both time and space into sacred. According to the authors, rituals can *re-create and re-found the world, re-sacralizing time and beginning it anew, so that each ritual restores freshness and strength to a worn-out world*. Rituals also sacralize environment, including the objects and people in them. In other words, without rituals, both time and space cannot become sacred.

With this analysis in mind, and for purposes of this book, we will define sacred as time and space that, using rituals:

- Transcends the ordinary
- Restores our freshness and strength

- Unifies those who share in the rituals

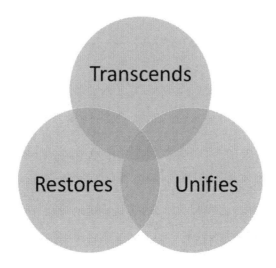

**Figure i** - The definition of sacred has three elements we will apply to the workday.

If we translate this concept to the workday, the definition of profane should come as no surprise. In a recent study, only 51% of Americans said they were satisfied with their jobs; and those were only so due to lowered expectations: *the higher satisfaction levels may reflect declining expectations among workers.*[2] This sentiment is a tragedy when you consider that most people spend **more than one-third of their time at work**. The adverse effect of being unsatisfied at work is that you bring that dissatisfaction home with you and, before you know it, the remaining two-thirds of your time spent with family, friends or sleeping also begins to lose its sanctity.

We only get 24 hours in a day. This book provides a how-to guide to performing the rituals needed to make your 8-hour workday sacred: transcending the ordinary, restoring freshness and strength, and unifying those who share in the rituals. But there is an interesting phenomenon that will occur when the rituals in this book are followed: the remaining 16 hours will also become sacred. *How?* Let's consider the following example.

To me, a gym is a sacred place. When I go to the gym, I transcend the ordinary by testing my physical and mental capabilities, as opposed to sitting on my couch and unwinding after a hard day's work as most people do. I restore my freshness and strength, even though I'm exerting myself. I feel unified with all those around me also performing rituals of self-improvement. Every time I go to this sacred place, I return to my family a better man: fulfilled, energic, and elevated. As a result, the quality of my time with them also improves and becomes more sacred.

**Figure ii** - When your workday becomes sacred, your time with your family, and sleeping become more sacred.

Simon Sinek, British-American author, motivational speaker and marketing consultant, discusses the importance of starting with the *why*. In doing so, he says you attract people to your organization who believe what you believe. He states, *such people work for you with blood, sweat, and tears.*[3] To me, there is no more compelling *why* than to make the 8 hours we spend at work sacred so that we can become better people for our customers, the people we care for, and, ultimately, ourselves.

In writing this book, I have sacrificed countless hours that could have been spent with my wife and children. It has not been easy. However, there is a Vision that has gotten me through it all. As I write this book, I am in the process of searching for a company to buy. It excites me to know that, very soon, I will be putting the rituals in this book to use at a business that I own, and that my employees will experience a Sacred Workday first-hand as many of my clients have. It is equally as exciting to know that there are those who will read this book and share the same experience. That higher purpose has transcended this book beyond writing an ordinary business book. The ritual of writing it has materialized my learnings into the written word and, in doing so, has restored my freshness and strength. It has also unified me to a group of people I have yet to meet or may never meet at all. To all of you reading this, welcome to this sacred space and join me in saying goodbye to the profane!

Daniel Custódio

# INTRODUCTION

## A PROFANE WORK DAY

If we are going to create a Sacred Workday, it's essential we dissect the profane one first.

The image below is a representation of a typical organization with the few decision-makers at the top and most frontline employees that deliver value to the customers at "the bottom."

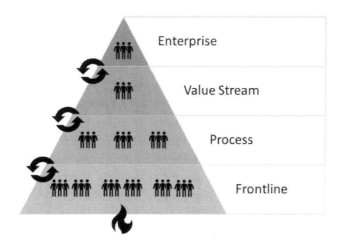

**Figure iii** - In any business, the frontlines are closest to the work and, thus, suffer the brunt of working for a system that does not know how to deal with problems in a structured way.

It is at the latter where frontline employees first encounter problems and most experience the profane, i.e., overburden, blame, and a general sense of dissatisfaction. They bear the brunt of the suffering.

In the absence of a system that allows for structured problem solving by the frontline employees, the modus operandum quickly becomes to escalate problems to management desperately. One effect of this is that employees bombard leadership with issues that take them away from critical strategic activity. The other result is that they most likely will make the situation worse.

As the image on the previous page depicts, leadership does not perform the work and, thus, is ill-equipped to come up with solutions. In the case where leaders understand their limitations, they ignore problems. As problems remain unresolved, the frontline employees grow disillusioned with leadership and escalate fewer and fewer issues. Ultimately, they are left to fend for themselves. Some frontline employees come up with creative ways to work around these problems, but most suffer silently.

The second scenario is even worse. Some leaders draw a false sense of power from their title. As such, they leverage an old-fashioned style of management referred to as *command and control,* also known as *do as I say!* Employees know these orders will not work but follow them regardless. Because leadership has not cultivated trust, there is very little upward communication. When things go awry, employees hide problems from leadership in fear. As a result, the administration is never equipped with adequate information to make informed decisions. Although they can smell the smoke or see the fire, they are clueless as to the root-causes.

In the rare case that management can come up with a solution, by the time they communicate that solution downward, the damage has already been done. The adverse effect of this outcome is that the majority closest to the work, who most likely have the hidden answers, become dependent on the few who most likely don't.

The good news is that there are rituals that have been around for quite some time that can move us from this profane work environment to a sacred one; from a work day that resents and hides problems, to a sacred one where we *perform unifying rituals that embrace problems and transform them into continuous improvement, thus, restoring employee freshness and strength.* Let's explore how.

> A Sacred Workday is one where we *perform unifying rituals that embrace problems and transform them into continuous improvement, thus, restoring employee freshness and strength.*

## A SACRED WORK DAY

> *If we were to respond to difficult situations with a positive or peaceful mind, they would not be problems for us; indeed, we may even come to regard them as challenges or opportunities for growth and development.*[4]

As the Buddha said in the first noble truth, *suffering does exist.*

Once we accept this (in other words, stop ignoring our suffering), the remaining three noble truths (there is a cause of your suffering, it is possible to eliminate suffering, and there is a path to eliminate suffering) focus on using suffering as the fuel that enables enlightenment. Those of you who have experienced this understand the sacredness in doing so.

I have. In 2009, my first wife left me unexpectedly. At the time, it was emotionally devastating. But I embraced the suffering and saw it as an opportunity to become a better man. My rituals were the acts of writing and performing poetry. Only one year later, I found myself on a Broadway stage performing a poem about the experience, entitled, *Hooked*. The piece served as a battle cry to all those who had gone through a similar experience. My reaction to the tragic event was not typical. I could have crumbled, felt sorry for myself, or reacted with anger. But I didn't. The rituals of writing and performing poetry restored my freshness and strength, and unified me with those who listened to my poetry and took part in the ceremony.

With this concept becoming more widely accepted in popular culture, such as in Ryan Holiday's best-seller, *The Obstacle is the Way*, and applied at the personal level, why haven't more companies tapped into this power? The Tibetan Buddhist teacher, Geshe Kelsang Gyatso, provides us with additional insight:

> *When things go wrong in our life, and we encounter stressful situations, we tend to regard the situation itself as our problem, but in reality whatever problems we experience come from the side of the mind. If we were to respond to difficult situations with a positive or peaceful mind, they would not be problems for us; indeed, we may even come to regard them as challenges or opportunities for growth and development. Problems only arise if we respond to difficulties with a negative state of mind. Therefore, if we want to transform our lives and be free from problems, we must transform our mind.*[5]

As Gyatso points out, problems are not the problem, but, instead, how we react to those problems, i.e., our mindset.

As difficult as it may be to change the mindset, there is good news: it is not hard-wired. Recent studies by neuroscientists point out that the brain is adaptable - a concept known as *neuroplasticity*.[6] By replacing old habits with new ones, we can start to alter the way we think. Thus, the key to changing mindset comes down to the patterns we form. Habits can be destructive or "bad habits," e.g., going to bed late, eating the wrong foods, or watching too much television. In this case, they lead to the profane. Habits can also be useful or rituals. In this case, they transform the sacrilegious to sacred.

Thus, it is clear why more companies cannot achieve a Sacred Workday: they lack the rituals, and, therefore, cannot develop the proper mindset that embraces problems. Such companies have failed to learn from a set of routines that have been refined by Toyota.

## LEAN RITUALS

For eighteen years I have been a student and teacher of a philosophy popularized by Toyota called *Lean*. According to the Lean Enterprise Institute (LEI), the term Lean was coined to describe Toyota's business during the late 1980s by a research team headed by Jim Womack, Ph.D., at MIT's International Motor Vehicle Program.[7] There are many definitions of Lean, but, as it relates to this book, I define it as *the unifying rituals we perform that embrace problems and transform them into continuous improvement, thus, restoring employee freshness and strength.*

Taiichi Ohno, a Japanese Industrial Engineer who worked for Toyota and famous for shaping the Lean philosophy, said that an organization should mimic the reflex arc in the human body. If you were to place your hand on a hot surface accidentally, your reflex arc would respond by pulling your hand away immediately to minimize the damage. This reaction happens faster than it takes for the pain signal to reach your brain and back to your hand (next time this happens to you, note how you pull your hand away before registering the pain). By doing so, you avoid further damage.

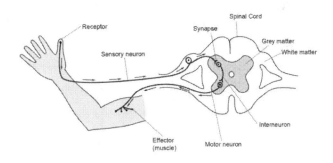

**Figure ix** - Diagram to display the reflex arc.[8]

Similarly, in Ohno's model, rather than escalate problems and wait helplessly, the frontline employees are empowered with the autonomy to respond to issues quickly and methodically by enacting countermeasures, acting as a business's reflex arc. My rule of thumb is that every company should strive to have 80% of all problems resolved by the frontlines employees and their managers. When issues cannot be addressed timely, a tool called an *Andon* light, which we will further explore later in this book, is leveraged to escalate problems to leadership quickly. However, rather than send issues to an office where a leader sits idly waiting, leaders go to the problems at the *genba* (the place work happens), another concept we will further explore later, ready to learn and help when appropriate. This form of servant leadership begins to eliminate the divide that often exists between those who do the work and those who manage it. If leaders do this right, the result is a sacred trust (sacred because it transcends the ordinary, unifies two groups that are often in opposition although they work for the same business, and, as a result, restores freshness and strength).

In sharp contrast to the bad habits of low performing companies, high performing companies create armies of problem solvers who are empowered by servant leaders. Employees are self-disciplined, self-accountable and, most importantly, coached and developed by their managers. As a result, their workday becomes sacred. The competition is rendered helpless.

This book provides us with a formula on how to implement the rituals required to create a Sacred Workday and to make Ohno's vision a reality. Each day is a new one, and it is easy for us not to perform the rituals and for old habits to reemerge. We will now explore a framework that will allow us to avoid such entropy gifted to us by a man named Shigeo Shingo.

## THE SHINGO MODEL

Shigeo Shingo, like Ohno, was also a Japanese Industrial Engineer who worked for Toyota, and who also contributed a tremendous amount to Lean thinking. One of the critical frameworks I use in this book is inspired by him and known as the *Shingo Model*™, as seen below.

This model is an elevated one that goes beyond the unfortunate tool-thinking that permeates the broader Lean community.

In this model, there are three key insights (for purposes of this book, I have replaced the term behavior with ritual as they are synonymous):

- Ideal results require ideal rituals
- Purpose and systems drive rituals
- Principles inform ideal rituals

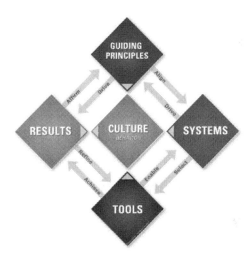

**Figure v** - A representation of the Shingo Model™ framework.[9]

What this is saying is that ideal results (those that are sustainable) require rituals that are proven and grounded in principles that are universally true. In doing so, we ensure that our rituals will yield the desired effects. If the rituals are not grounded in principles that are universally true, then they will undoubtedly fail and, as a result, employees will lose faith in them. However, once we establish the right rituals, we must turn our attention to ensuring we follow them. As the Shingo Model™ states, this won't just happen. People need purpose and systems that drive the execution of the desired rituals. If the rituals do not occur, we must question whether employees understand the purpose and improve our system until they do. As a practicing Zen Buddhist, let me offer a simple example.

As mentioned above, the Buddha introduced the Four Noble Truths: suffering exists, there is a cause of your suffering, it is possible to eliminate suffering, and there is a path to eliminate suffering. The Buddha referred to them as *noble* because they are universal. In other words, Christians, Hindus, and even Atheists would agree with the fact that we all suffer, there is a root-cause to our suffering, it is possible to eliminate suffering (even if, ultimately, via death), and there is a path to eliminate suffering. Meditation is an ideal ritual grounded in these truths and has a growing body of scientific evidence that demonstrates its' efficacy in ending suffering.[10] And, indeed, there are those who practice a wide range of religions and find peace in meditation. However, even as a practicing Buddhist who knows the impact of this ideal ritual, I still fail to meditate without reminding myself of the purpose and the use of a system. For me, the aim is to become a better man for all of those who are a part of my life. For me, that system consists of a series of tools (an alarm to signal the start of meditation, a cushion to sit comfortably, and prayer beads to time my meditation) that interact in a way that ensures the ritual will take place. If we do not achieve the desired result, the tools and methods can be adjusted; in other words, if we do not perform the ritual, we experiment with the system until we can achieve it. Because the routine is grounded in truth, we don't give up on it. We can easily translate this lesson to the creation of a Sacred Workday.

In this book, we will introduce the 10 Shingo principles and a series of unifying rituals grounded in these principles that will allow us to achieve a Sacred Workday. We will also further explore our purpose and discuss the systems needed to ensure we consistently perform these rituals until they become culture. There will be little emphasis on tools. There are plenty of Lean books on tools out there, but few focus on how to create systems that ensure we *perform unifying rituals that embrace problems and transform them into continuous improvement, thus, restoring freshness and strength.*

My formula consists of 10 parts as depicted in the visual of the torii below. These parts include:

1. Building Trust
2. Ideal Results
3. Ideal Behaviors
4. Enterprise-level Production System
5. Enterprise-level Management System
6. Value stream-level Production System
7. Value stream-level Management System
8. Process-level Production System
9. Process-level Management System
10. Rituals

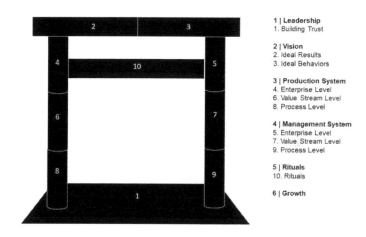

**Figure vi** - The different components that make up a Sacred Workday and that also make up the chapters of this book depicted as a torii.

Anyone can be hired to build any one of these parts in isolation. However, if those parts cannot come together in a precise manner, a Sacred Workday will never be achieved and what will result can be seen in the image on the next page. At the tool level, a business may even appear to be strong. However, when problems arise – and they always will – that business will not be able to survive. To those who follow the recipe in this book, not only will you survive, but you will thrive.

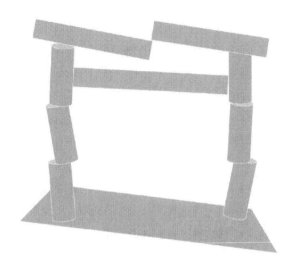

**Figure vii** - A business that does not bring together all the elements in a precise manner will not be able to achieve a Sacred Workday.

# SUMMARY OF CHAPTERS

**Chapter 1** focuses on **leadership**. Specifically, we will explore what it means to be a leader in the construct of a Sacred Workday. As demonstrated in the picture of our torii on the previous page, if we do not build our business on stable ground, the entire structure will be compromised. If leadership does not have the right mindset, they will never achieve a Sacred Workday. As a result, it is critical that leadership be the first to practice and role-model the unifying rituals to demonstrate their importance and to build trust amongst the employees. In this chapter, we will take a deeper dive into how to do so using a technique known as *Humble Inquiry*.

**Chapter 2** focuses on **Vision**. Vision consists of both ideal results and ideal behaviors. In that chapter, we will discuss how to define ideal results by focusing on a few, key measures. We will then take a deep dive into the 10 Shingo principles used to identify the ideal rituals needed to drive us towards our ideal results.

**Chapter 3** focuses on **Production System**. In this chapter, we will introduce superior production archetypes used to deliver value to customers. We will discuss what the Production System looks like at each level of the business, from the enterprise level to the process level, highlighting the interdependencies at each level that create alignment. In keeping with the theme of Lean leadership introduced in chapter 1, we will start at the enterprise level where rituals must begin.

**Chapter 4** focuses on **Management System**. When using superior production archetypes to deliver value to customers, we will also require superior management archetypes to manage the delivery of this value. In this chapter, we will discuss the five elements of our Management System: *Standard Work, Sensory Management, Self-*

*Accountability, Self-Discipline*, and, last, but certainly not least, *Coaching and Development*. Like the Production System, we will also discuss what the Management System looks like at each level of the business so that we can even manage in an aligned way.

**Chapter 5** focuses on **rituals**. In the first four chapters, we focused on creating a blueprint for a Sacred Workday. In this chapter, we transition to the rituals that will allow us to move from potential to kinetic, from the profane to the sacred. As we will explore, these rituals happen at different levels of the organization at different intervals. Although the content will move from more strategic to more tactical as we move from the enterprise level to the process one, the rituals, themselves, will remain the same. The specific routines we will focus on will include the following: the formation of alignment throughout the enterprise to ensure everyone is moving in the same direction towards our Vision; how to break-down the Vision into less intimidating parts called *Challenges* and *Target Conditions* that everyone can strive towards; and the daily and intra-daily cycles of experimentation needed to take steps towards creating a Sacred Workday.

Lastly, **chapter 6** focuses on **growth**. Specifically, we will discuss how to expand our initial efforts to create a Sacred Workday for the entire business. We will also discuss the common pitfalls that sabotage a Sacred Workday and explain how to avoid this.

# 1 | LEADERSHIP

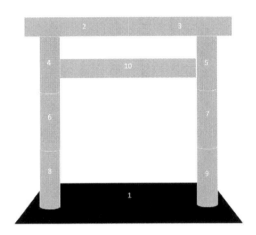

1 | Leadership
1. Building Trust

2 | Vision
2. Ideal Results
3. Ideal Behaviors

3 | Production System
4. Enterprise Level
6. Value Stream Level
8. Process Level

4 | Management System
5. Enterprise Level
7. Value Stream Level
9. Process Level

5 | Rituals
10. Rituals

6 | Growth

## BUILDING TRUST

If we are to create a Sacred Workday, we need to explore further how to do so. After all, this sort of culture doesn't just happen. It requires leadership that wants to do it and has the know-how.

In my experience, even after we create a system that mimics the reflex arc, which we will explore in the subsequent chapters, employees struggle with being given such autonomy. As explored in the introduction, when leadership has historically used command-and-control to manage, their employees adopt a mindset of submission and fear. This way of thinking isn't easy to change. When given autonomy, employees don't know what to do with it. They are either skeptical about managements true intentions or don't believe in their capabilities as problem solvers because they have never exercised such skills. In the infamous movie, *Shawshank*

*Redemption*, Morgan Freeman (Red) describes inmates' feelings towards prison:

> *These walls are funny. First, you hate 'em, then you get used to 'em. Enough time passes, you get so you depend on them. That's institutionalized.*[11]

Although it may seem a dramatic comparison, is it that far off? I have met countless employees who say they hate their job, yet, when given the opportunity to leave for something better, they cower and stay put citing their need for money to send their children to private school or convincing themselves that *it's just not that bad after all*. Their companies have institutionalized them. Changing such a culture is not easy. It requires a deliberate pivot in how leadership behaves: they need to permit employees to be autonomous, coach them on how to be so, and build trust.

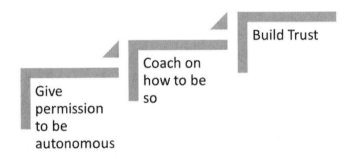

Figure 1.1 - Steps that transition us from a fear culture to one where employees behave like the reflex arc.

Edgar H. Schein offers a powerful tool that allows leaders to build this trust called *Humble Inquiry*. In Schein's book, *Humble Inquiry*, he states the following:

> *The world is becoming more technologically complex, interdependent, and culturally diverse, which makes the building of relationships more and more necessary to get*

*things accomplished and, at the same time, more difficult.*[12]

In our society and within businesses, people rely on one another to complete tasks. Our ability to build a relationship with each other will impact how well we accomplish those tasks. This logic makes sense when you think about your personal life. If you are kind and build repour with the customer service representative on the phone, they are more likely to try and go above-and-beyond to help you out. However, if you are irritated and short with them (as if they had anything to do with the primary reason you are calling about) and don't take time to get to know them as a person, they are less likely to accomplish what you want, how you want it. Humble Inquiry allows you to build that repour.

Schein defines Humble Inquiry as:

*A behavior that comes out of respect, genuine curiosity, and the desire to improve the quality of the conversation by stimulating greater openness and the sharing of task-relevant information.*

He further defines it by stating,

*Humble Inquiry does not influence either the content of what the other person has to say or the form in which it is said.*

To Schein, Humble Inquiry is not a check-list or pre-written questions to choose from. Instead, Humble Inquiry is a mindset (there is that word again). When adopted it enables higher level conversations that, in turn, allow us to accomplish tasks better. It's all about making the need to complete a job subservient to personalization, what Schein defines as *the process of acknowledging the other person as a whole human; not just a role.*

If we return to the example with the customer service representation, you may start off the conversation with, *how are you?* According to Stein, your initial question is *not* Humble Inquiry because this question is commonplace and doesn't demonstrate genuine curiosity. However, if the customer service representative replies by saying they are not having a good day and you respond by saying, *I'm sorry to hear that, how come?*, with a tone of concern, this *is* a form of Humble Inquiry. Your response demonstrates care, genuine curiosity, and, more importantly, puts the initial reason you called to the side. You have acknowledged the person on the other end of that phone as human. Your question could be the difference between that person on the other end of the phone having a good day or bad one. It will also improve the chances you will receive excellent service. So, although it takes more time initially than it would if you cut-to-the-chase, it saves more time in the long-run. In Lean, this is often referred to as *go slow to go fast*.

In our business, it is essential for leadership to use Humble Inquiry to promote frontline employees act like the reflex arc. For example, when a problem occurs, the following questions by leadership are not good examples of Humble Inquiry:

- Have you considered the following root-cause?
- Have you thought about implementing the following countermeasure?

Both questions are biased and trying to influence the frontline employee to take a specific action and think a certain way. If there is a lack of trust, employees will follow the leaders' suggestion and, as we explored in the introduction, the proposal will, most likely, yield little value, i.e., the profane.

More appropriate questions that would demonstrate Humble Inquiry when coupled with genuine interest would be:

- What do you know about the problem?
- What have you already done to try and solve the problem?
- What did you learn?
- What is your next step?

All these questions empower the employee to be self-accountable and to take ownership.

There are three other forms of inquiry Schein brings up, and they are *diagnostic, confrontational,* and *process-oriented*:

1. Diagnostic inquiry influences mental processes (feelings and reactions, causes and motives, action-oriented, systemic questions).
2. Confrontational inquiry inserts your ideas in the form of a question. This form of investigation requires a high level of trust.
3. Process-oriented inquiry shifts the focus of the questions onto the conversation itself, e.g., how do you feel this conversation is going?

Although these forms of inquiry can be used and may even get to the intended result quicker, in my opinion, there are two reasons why Humble Inquiry is superior:

1. It puts the leader in learner mode and ensures any forms of bias don't pollute the conversation.
2. It places the person asked in a position of ownership.

There are times when leaders will need to be directive, especially when it comes to setting the Vision and systems we will use to operate as a business. However, when it comes to the work performed by the frontlines and problem solving related to that work, I strongly recommend always using Humble Inquiry as the standard, regardless of how much trust you have established.

For leaders who want some strategies on how to become better at Humble Inquiry, Schein offers the following table on the next page:

| # | Strategy | Explanation |
|---|----------|-------------|
| 1 | Slow down / vary pace | In a task-driven world, we operate fast; often at the expense of trust. It's important to slow down if to cultivate relationships. |
| 2 | Reflect more and ask yourself Humble Inquiry questions | Like any new skill set, Humble Inquiry takes practice. Although Humble Inquiry is not a set of questions, it's helpful to come up with some questions that will help you during your interactions. Doing so will allow you to focus more on intention and authenticity. |
| 3 | Become more mindful | Mindfulness means being present in the moment. When you are with a person, be there. Don't let your mind wander to the next meeting or your to-do list. |
| 4 | Try innovating and engage the artist in you | When people have interests outside of work, they become more interesting. These interests can be a point of connecting with other employees. |
| 5 | Review and reflect on your behavior after an event | Again, Humble Inquiry is not something we do naturally. There will be times when you revert to old habits. After each event, reflect and think about how you can improve. |
| 6 | Become sensitive to coordination needs in your network | As we will discuss later in this book, an organization is a network and people within that network are dependent on each other. By being sensitive to those dependencies as a leader, you can focus on where stronger ties need to exist, e.g., sales and operations. |

| 7 | As a leader, build relationships | Great leaders bring people together and build trust in the broader community. |
| 8 | Create culture islands | By creating fun events outside of work; employees can get to know each other in a different context, providing an essential opportunity for team building. |

Why does all this matter?

As we dive into what a Sacred Workday looks and feels like, the theme of leaders going to the work to understand will be prevalent. If leaders don't know how to have conversations with employees and build trust, employees will resent their arrival. However, if leaders use Humble Inquiry, employees will welcome them. Leaders will discover things about their business they never knew. They will free their employees to come up with ways to overcome problems, and they will be able to get involved and help solve where appropriate. For those leaders, they will feel more valuable than they ever have in their entire lives and they will never want to revert to their old way of "leading" ever again.

## WHO IS A LEADER?

It is vital that leadership be early adopters and role model the behavior they wish to see in others. Anything less would be hypocrisy. It is only natural that people imitate their leaders; culture trickles downwards.

However, it is essential to clarify that everyone in our business should view themselves as a leader. As the picture on the next page demonstrates, in any business, there is some hierarchy. In that hierarchy, the person at the top should lead their direct reports and their direct reports should do the same with theirs, and so on and so forth. Although the frontline employees may not have direct reports, they still should serve as leaders to their peers, i.e., a more seasoned employee should train a new one on the ideal rituals.

As a result, it is essential that those who are not managers focus on this chapter as well. If our business is to achieve a Sacred Workday where we *perform unifying rituals that embrace problems and transform them into continuous improvement, thus, restoring employee freshness and strength,* everyone must adopt the mindset of Humble Inquiry to create the needed trust that will form our foundation.

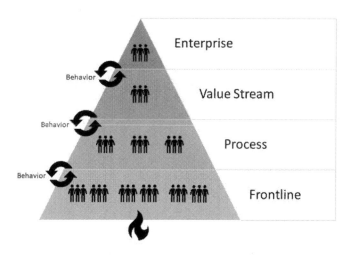

**Figure 1.2** - Although leaders at the enterprise level must be the first to role-model Humble Inquiry, everyone in our business should view themselves as a leader and work on developing trust vertically and horizontally.

# 1 | SUMMARY

- Traditional command-and-control management has adverse effects on employees, creating an institutionalized mindset grounded in submission and fear.
- Leaders, starting from the top, have a direct responsibility to permit employees to be autonomous, coach them on how to be so, and build trust.
- Humble Inquiry is the primary tool to create trust; it allows for higher quality conversations, which, in turn, enables us to complete tasks better.
- Because Humble Inquiry does not come naturally and is a new skill, we need to practice.
- Although leaders at the top need to role-model the behavior they desire, everyone in the organization should view themselves as leaders and practice Humble Inquiry as a way of creating trust throughout the organization.

# 1 | EXERCISE

I borrowed many of these exercises from Ed Schein's book, *Humble Inquiry*.

Reflect on the following questions.

- What is your leadership style?
- What are the dependencies you have on others in our business?
- Think of a situation when your boss made you feel respected. How did they do that?
- Reflect on what kind of questions you ask and how this influences the trust in your relationships.
- If you were to build more of a trusting relationship with one of direct reports or peers, how would you go about doing it? How personal would you be willing to be?

# 2 | VISION

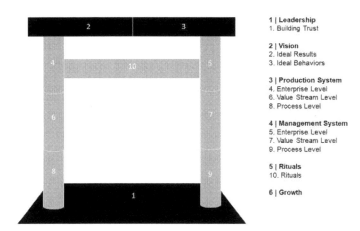

1 | Leadership
1. Building Trust

2 | Vision
2. Ideal Results
3. Ideal Behaviors

3 | Production System
4. Enterprise Level
6. Value Stream Level
8. Process Level

4 | Management System
5. Enterprise Level
7. Value Stream Level
9. Process Level

5 | Rituals
10. Rituals

6 | Growth

Merriam-Webster defines visionary as *having or marked by foresight and imagination.*[13] Visionaries see the world through a different lens. When all others see the ordinary and profane, visionaries see what could be extraordinary and sacred. When all others see the muddy swamp, visionaries know that those are the conditions from which the lotus emerges.

In 2015, my wife and I built our first home. When we purchased the land, our relatives thought we were crazy. The land we bought was wild, inhabited by mosquitos, and seemed to be uninhabitable. But we had a Vision of what could be: a green home on 7-acres of our very own little forest where our kids could be one with nature. A year later, we made that Vision a reality, and our relatives couldn't believe it. They saw the profane. We saw the sacred.

As leaders, we must use our imagination and see a Sacred Workday before it exists. But equally as important, if not more so, we need to share this Vision in a way that allows everyone to see it as clearly as we do. But before that, we must be clear on our purpose.

| Before | After |

**Figure 2.1** - A before picture of the land we bought and an after image of the home we built on that land in 2015.

## PURPOSE

The Japanese have a word, *ikigai* (生き甲斐), which translates into *a reason for being or a reason for getting up in the morning.*[14] A Sacred Workday is not easy to achieve; it requires a tremendous amount of intelligence, wisdom, and discipline. If our employees don't have ikigai, they will not have the resolve to help achieve a Sacred Workday, and they will revert to the profane along the way. So, what is a purpose that will get our employees out of bed and ready to strive towards a Sacred Workday?

In the introduction, we stated that our compelling *why* was to achieve a Sacred Workday to make the 8 hours we spend at work sacred so that we can become a better person for our customers, the people we care for, and, ultimately, ourselves.

This is a very compelling *why*, but, in my experience, isn't enough for all employees. The reality is, the concept of a Sacred Workday, in-and-of-itself, seems too theoretical. People are more grounded in the notion of job security and being able to pay their bills. Again, we can turn to Toyota for a history lesson.

Taiichi Ohno made two practical promises to employees when first introducing the concepts of Lean:

1. Employees were given a job for life and
2. Profits were shared with employees

When introducing Lean, be cautious, as many employees fear the loss of their jobs due to realized efficiencies. Ohno removed this concern, which, in turn, incentivized employees to be creative. The second promise needs no explanation. With these promises in place, employees ikigai goes from merely getting a check to improving their business and thriving.

Building upon the lessons learned by Toyota, we add onto our compelling why and make it even stronger by defining our purpose as three-fold:

1. To make the 8 hours we spend at work sacred so that we can become better people for our customers, the people we care for, and, ultimately, ourselves;
2. To share the rewards (financial and non-financial) that a Sacred Workday generates with our employees and customers; and
3. To provide a job for life to all those who will want to participate in creating a Sacred Workday.

Although simple, in theory, most businesses do not make this their purpose due to greed, lack of skill, or both.

When employees understand that their leadership is serious about a purpose which includes helping them thrive as human beings as well, they will be ready to listen to your Vision.

## TWO ELEMENTS OF VISION

Now that we have defined our purpose, it is time to create and share our Vision. According to the first Shingo Model™ insight, ideal results require ideal rituals. Thus, our Vision should consist of both these parts.

### IDEAL RESULTS

Business needs to financially thrive to create wealth for everyone involved if we are going to realize our purpose. Thus, we also need to be visionary about the results we want to achieve. There are many key performance indicators we can monitor to ensure that we are financially healthy. I like to focus on two:

1. Revenue

2. Gross margin $= \dfrac{\text{(Revenue} - \text{Cost of Goods Sold or COGS)}}{\text{Revenue}}$

You can measure net profit margin, operating margin, debt/equity ratio and quick ratio. However, I find that, through the creation of a Sacred Workday, we can increase capacity (thus, allowing us to grow revenue) and create efficiencies (therefore, improving gross margins). As a result, we can allocate more money to paying off debts, general and administrative expenses, interest expenses and distributions to shareholders and employees. When businesses have financial issues, they often resort to drastic measures such as cutting wages or layoffs in a desperate attempt to impact their numbers positively. Although these measures may help the business in the short-term, in the long-term, it hurts trust and stunts any potential for growth.

For both revenue and gross margin, it is essential we first analyze the current state. What is the current performance of both metrics? What have the trends been? Once we do this, we make a 5-year projection for each one of these, with year-over-year targets specified.

This exercise is partially a mathematical one and can be done using an excel spreadsheet. The other part uses the imagination.

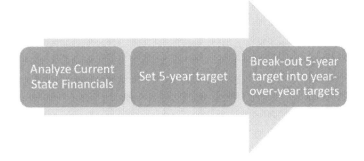

**Figure 2.2** - Three steps needed to set the financial part of the Vision.

I find it helpful to use the expression, *wouldn't it be nice if...* to encourage the creation of targets that are truly visionary. Another phrase that is helpful to use is, *what do we need the 5-year projection to be?* My preference is for the later as it creates a sense of urgency. It's not a matter of *if*, but *how*. In other words, what problems do we need to overcome to make the 5-year projection a reality?

Once we do this, it is important we consider our various product and service offerings and how they are performing to these metrics. We then need to discuss our strategy for each. The matrix on the next page provides a guide to help us think through these strategies.

For example, if we have a product line that accounts for high gross margins, but low revenue, we should consider increasing our sales for the product through a concentrated marketing effort. In doing so, we would need to create the required operational capacity to do so.

As you will see in subsequent chapters, a Sacred Workday will improve gross margins. Thus, if we have a product line that accounts for high revenue, but low gross margin, we should consider prioritizing it and beginning our efforts to create a Sacred Workday there.

It would be helpful to use some additional tools such as industry analysis and voice of the customer analysis to better define our strategy.

For example, industry analysis might indicate whether there is an opportunity for growth or not by understanding whether the market, in general, is growing, and by understanding what our market share is in comparison to our competitors.

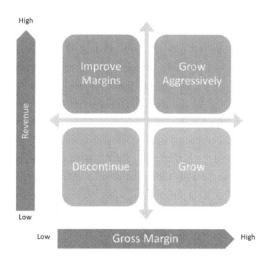

**Figure 2.3** - A simple matrix used to determine a strategy for each of our product and services.

S.W.O.T. (Strengths Weaknesses Opportunities Threats) analysis is another useful tool in understanding the current state of our business to formulate a strategy to steal market share.

Customer focus groups could provide us with valuable insights into what customers feel about our products and services, which, in turn, could inform our strategy. Too many companies fail to gather this information and view their company from the inside-out, rather than from the outside-in. These blinders are very dangerous, and we should not make the same mistake if we are to achieve a Sacred Workday indeed.

Once our ideal results are defined, it's essential that we change gears and focus on ideal rituals. Unfortunately, most businesses would stop at ideal results. They convey these results to their management team, and everyone begins to charge towards the target (typically, blindly and fearfully). The problem with this is that they can achieve the objectives using very profane behaviors. Even worse, there may be incentive structures in place that encourage or reward such harmful practices. That is why it is equally as important to define how we want people to behave as they strive to achieve the ideal results. Let's look at how to do so.

## IDEAL RITUALS

The Shingo Institute defines culture as behavior. Mike Orzen, a Lean practitioner and Shingo-award-winning author, describes behavior as something that can be videotaped and observed. A lot of businesses publicize their culture via expensive posters at the workplace. However, if you were to follow their employees, you would not see rituals consistent with that desired culture. In fact, most companies would be embarrassed by the results of the captured behavior: gossip behind closed doors, arguments, lengthy meetings where employees multi-task on laptops because they feel like management is wasting their time, etc. That begs the question, what are the ideal Lean rituals needed to create a Sacred Workday? The Shingo Model™ offers ten guiding principles as seen on the next page to help us develop the answer this question.

If you recall our introduction, a principle is synonymous with truth. The litmus test is as follows: *when stated, no person can dispute it or disagree with it.* When we think about world religions, the principle of *love thy neighbor* is a universally accepted truth. No one can argue against it.

Unfortunately, our society often polarizes people by taking the focus away from principles and, instead, concentrates on the superficial differences that, in theory, should not divide us. This foolishness is synonymous to the tool-thinking described in our introduction. Principles act as the foundation of culture and will help us define our ideal rituals. As such, they deserve a deeper dive.

**Figure 2.4** - The 10 Shingo Principles broken out into four categories: Results, Enterprise Alignment, Continuous Improvement, and Cultural Enablers.

## Results: Create Value for the Customer

Businesses exist to provide a product and service that adds value to their customers. As a result, it is essential to understand how your customers define value. Too many businesses assume they know what their customers want, but they haven't taken the time to find out. Even worse, some employees speak of the customer as if they are the enemy! How can you resent the very people who help you pay your bills? As absurd as this may seem, we understand why this happens. Due to the stresses employees in a profane work environment are forced to endure, rather than embrace problems that arise in the form of customer complaints, employees begin to resent customers. This attitude leads to such profane behavior as yelling at customers. Although customers should never have the right to act disrespectful, they do have the right to be upset when the value we promise them is not delivered, and we should embrace each time that happens as an opportunity to learn and continuously improve.

## Enterprise Alignment: Create Constancy of Purpose

Constancy of Purpose is when everyone in a business is working towards the same Vision and understand how their specific role contributes towards making the idea a reality.

Championship sports teams role model this very well. Take basketball, for example. There are five players on a team, and each has a specific focus. Collectively, however, they are working towards the same Vision. They must act in a coordinated fashion to achieve it.

The picture below outlines how an organization creates alignment in a business through a process called *Hoshin* (Japanese for alignment) *Planning* and *Catch-Ball*, which we will discuss in chapter 5 on rituals. At the enterprise level, leaders create the Vision. That Vision then cascades down to the next level in the organization called the *value stream*, which we will further explore in the next chapter on the Production System.

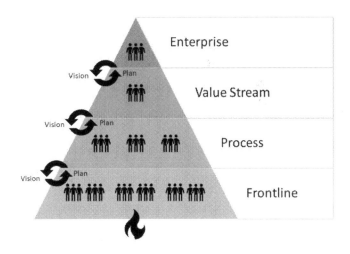

**Figure 2.5** - Leadership creates constancy of purpose when Vision cascades down and then is translated into a plan and operationalized by the receiving group. This process, known as Hoshin Planning and Catch-Ball, is repeated until we reach the frontline.

Once the value stream manager understands the intended direction, their job is to respond with how the value stream will achieve the expected direction. This process continues all the way to the frontline employees who deliver the value. What cascades down is always the intended direction, not answers on how to achieve it. This guideline encourages those closest to the work to shape how to run the business. In doing so, employees become vested in the company.

### Enterprise Alignment: Think Systemically

Think Systemically is about understanding the relationships and interconnectedness within a system. In doing so, leaders can make better decisions that benefit the whole and not just the part. Any hand-off in a process is a point in the system more susceptible to failure. By thinking systemically, businesses begin to understand their value streams better and run their business horizontally through the lens of the customer, rather than vertically through the single lens of the shareholders.

### Continuous Improvement: Flow and Pull Value

Flow is the continuous delivery of value. We should always strive for this principle, even when it seems impossible to achieve. When flow is not possible, we want to ensure that downstream processes pull from upstream ones to ensure we only produce what is needed when it is required. This method is known as *just-in-time* (abbreviated as *JIT*) and is more difficult to achieve than it sounds as most businesses fall prey to the eight wastes (*muda* in Japanese), which we will further explore in the next chapter on the Production System.

### Continuous Improvement: Assure Quality at the Source

We should deal with defects where defects happen: at the source.

Unfortunately, too many times, mistakes are pushed forward for somebody else to handle. As a result, that somebody else must rework the error and that delays delivery of value to the customers. I'm reminded of this principle whenever I put a piece of furniture together and perform one of the steps incorrectly, i.e., place a piece on backward, only to discover it several steps later. As a result, I must undo what I have done, correct the mistake, and redo work. It is super frustrating and a waste of my time. Quality at the source is all about catching defects as they occur when they occur so that we don't waste time. The most significant obstacle to doing so is typically the lack of safety employees feel when it comes to stopping the line (our culture is one that promotes production, not slowing down or stopping). They think that quality at the source will result in blame, which leads us to our next principle.

### Continuous Improvement: Focus on the Process

Dr. W. Edwards Deming, an American engineer, statistician, professor, author, lecturer, and management consultant, stated that 85% of problems are a direct result of a poorly designed system by management. We could attribute the remaining 15% to human error.[15] As a result, it only makes sense that we focus on our system, rather than exerting our energy trying to blame people. The latter is not constructive given the percentage of errors that originate from the system designed by management. Focus on the process is a mindset of assuming problems are a direct result of a poorly designed system. We embrace the problem and seek to better understand the system and how we can improve it. This act is tough to do and works against our very nature of how we respond to problems as we will explore in chapter 4 on Management System. However, in doing so, people feel safe enough to bring up problems (the fuel for a Sacred Workday) as opposed to hiding them.

### Continuous Improvement: Embrace Scientific Thinking

I don't watch much television with my children, but when I do, one of my favorite shows to watch is the *Cosmos* hosted by Neil deGrasse Tyson. What astonishes me when I watch the show is how often those with power in our society have neglected science in the name of profit. This trend continues today with the topic of climate change. If we can't change, I'm afraid for my children because the world they will inherit will be a lot harsher.

Scientific thinking is about using observation and data to make decisions. We suspend all judgment and opinions and let the evidence do the talking, as they say. Hierarchy doesn't supersede logic.

Scientific thinking is also about learning. When leadership sets an aggressive Vision that is beyond what anyone has ever accomplished, the only way to get there is through experimentation. In Lean, we use the *Plan Do Check Adjust* or *PDCA cycle* (also introduced by Deming) to experiment. The business that wins will experiment quickly and often. In other words, they are not afraid to fail because each failure teaches a lesson and allows them to form a competitive advantage.

For example, in the two scenarios below, which would you bet money on? Scenario #2 is the obvious choice. In the same amount of time, the business in Scenario #2 has tried four experiments, while the business in scenario #1 has only attempted 1.

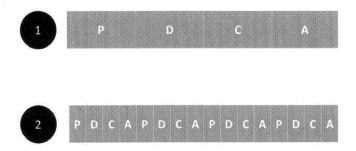

**Figure 2.6** - In the same amount of time, the business in scenario two has learned four times as much as the business in scenario 1.

## Continuous Improvement: Seek Perfection

*Seek* is the key word in this principle, which describes a mindset. It doesn't say *achieve*, which is a result. Seek perfection ensures that no matter how good you get, you always strive to get better. The most dangerous place to be is on top; to be "the best." It is precisely at that moment that complacency settles in and your competition surprises you. A business that has created a Sacred Workday never rests. They know that they can quickly revert to the profane in only a matter of a single day.

## Cultural Enablers: Lead with Humility

Humility is one of those overused, empty words. The word is often wrongly associated with weakness. However, humility is the exact opposite of weakness. It is the ultimate strength.

As Simon Sinek says,

> *Great leaders don't need to act tough. Their confidence and humility serve to underscore their toughness.*[16]

Humility enables learning. In demonstrating humility, you embrace that there is always something to learn from everyone, regardless of their socio-economic status, level of education, or any other superficial factors. If scientific thinking is applied, anyone in our business can come up with an idea for improvement, regardless of their title or where they reside in the organization.

There are no superior people. However, there are superior ideas: those that have been vetted using experimentation (and even those ideas quickly become inferior with further testing). This distinction is subtle, but one that we must remember.

Without humility, achieving a Sacred Workday is not possible.

## *Cultural Enablers: Respect Every Individual*

Unfortunately, respect is also one of those overused, empty words. Respect for every individual translates into more than just believing that every person can reach their full potential. Respect turns into playing an active part in helping people achieve their full potential. In a Sacred Workday, each employee a) understands what is expected of them, b) knows exactly where they stand relative to what is expected, and c) is coached and developed by their manager to achieve success. Unlike most businesses that have annual reviews where they provide their employees with a rating and batched feedback, in a business that consistently produces a Sacred Workday, leaders offer employees regular coaching to improve. In contrast to a traditional company, managers in a Sacred Workday culture are there to build their employees up and ensure they succeed. This responsibility is the ultimate form of respect.

### Defining Ideal Behaviors

Now that we have reviewed the 10 Shingo principles, it's time to put them to use and define what ideal rituals we want for our business. Remember, behavior is something that you can observe and videotape. If our business were a reality television show, what would it say about our culture? Would we be proud?

If most people are honest with themselves, they would not be. But we must remember that these behavioral problems are opportunities! We must embrace them. Once we do that, we can transition to transforming them into sacred rituals. The first step in doing so is to the define what ideal rituals we want. In other words, what is the standard? Without a standard, technically, there is no problem as employees don't know what bar to shoot for regarding how they conduct themselves.

Defining ideal rituals must be done at each level of the business: the enterprise level, the value stream level, the process level, and the frontline level. Nobody is exempt from ideal rituals. The executive team needs to lead the charge and define what these rituals should be. As we will explore later in this book, each level will then put a plan together on how they will achieve those rituals.

**Figure 2.7** - If our business was a reality television show, what would it say about our culture? Would we see the profane or the sacred?

To begin with, I recommend selecting at least three behaviors for each of the Shingo Model™ categories: Results, Enterprise Alignment, Continuous Improvement, and Cultural Enablers. This can be a challenging exercise, especially for those who have not had exposure to a Sacred Workday culture. I find that the following sentence structure is helpful: *To display [the principle] we [action that can be videotaped].*

Here are some excellent examples:

- To display the principle of create value for the customer, we collect voice of the customer at our Huddles from our employees and capture problems to work on during problem-solving sessions.
- To display the principle of quality at the source, we trigger an Andon signal when a problem is detected so that we can conduct root-cause analysis.
- To display the principle of constancy of purpose, we perform

value-stream mapping to create a Challenge for the entire value stream.

- To display the principle of respect every individual, we create development plans for our employees and conduct monthly one-on-one sessions with them to review their progress and provide coaching.

All these examples pass our litmus test because they could be videotaped and observed as if watching athletes on the field. All the above examples of rituals leverage elements of Lean that I will expose us to in the subsequent chapters, i.e., Lean Production System and Lean Management System. As a result, it would be difficult for employees without knowledge of Lean to define what ideal rituals would look like. This task requires the assistance of a *sensei* (translated as one who was born before and meaning someone capable of teaching Lean).

Once we have defined ideal rituals, it's essential to bring it all together and package the Vision to share with everyone in our business.

## BRINGING IT ALL TOGETHER

Although the Vision may be inspiring, the day-to-day problems will test our ability to keep the Vision front-and-center. As such, the use of Vision Boards will be paramount to harness the power of visualization and keep us motivated.

We create a Vision Board by asking participants to bring in magazines that they find to be inspirational and that reflect their interests, i.e., yoga, home improvement, cooking, etc. Participants then cut out images and words that remind them of the Vision of what our business is trying to achieve: both ideal results and ideal rituals. A rallying cry or phrase that summarizes the Vision can also be helpful.

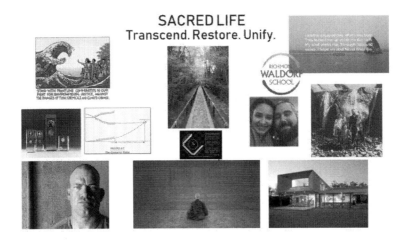

**Figure 2.8** - This is my family's Vision Board for five years out (2023). It should come as no surprise that my slogan is "sacred life."

The real value of a Vision Board is that it translates the ideal results (a dry topic for most) and ideal rituals into something more personalized that has a more significant impact on employees.

At this point, we have defined our Vision, and it's necessary to transition to a discussion on the two pillars that will help us make this Vision a reality: the Production System and the Management System.

# 2 | SUMMARY

- Sharing a company's purpose with its employees is critical.
- In a Sacred Workday culture, we add to our compelling why to create a stronger three-fold purpose:
    - To make the 8 hours we spend at work sacred so that we can become better people for our customers, the people we care for, and, ultimately, ourselves;
    - To share the rewards (financial and non-financial) that a sacred work day generates with our employees and customers; and
    - To provide a job for life to all those who will want to participate in creating a sacred work day
- There are two elements of Vision: ideal results and ideal rituals.
- Ideal results should focus on few, critical measures such as revenue and gross margin that will allow us to measure success.
- It is critical to understand the current state of how our business is performing to these measures and to set a Vision that is aspirational.
- Rituals are actions that can be video recorded.
- Ideal rituals should be defined using the 10 Shingo Principles as a guide.
- A Vision Board with a rallying cry is a great way to convey the Vision in an impactful way to employees.

# 2 | EXERCISE

- What is our company purpose? How does it compare to the purpose defined in this chapter? Should we make any modifications?
- If the behaviors in our company were videotaped (if we were on a reality television show) would we be proud?
- How would we describe our culture (behaviors that we observe)?
- Have we defined ideal results? If so, what are they? Is everyone in the business aware of what they are?
- Have we defined ideal rituals? If so, what are they? Is everyone in the business aware of what they are?

# 3 | PRODUCTION SYSTEM

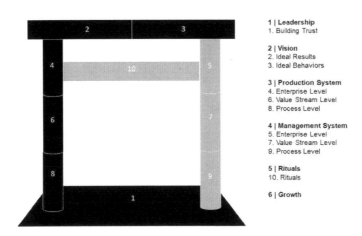

**1 | Leadership**
1. Building Trust

**2 | Vision**
2. Ideal Results
3. Ideal Behaviors

**3 | Production System**
4. Enterprise Level
6. Value Stream Level
8. Process Level

**4 | Management System**
5. Enterprise Level
7. Value Stream Level
9. Process Level

**5 | Rituals**
10. Rituals

**6 | Growth**

Although creating a Vision is a critical first step, the hard work needed to create a Sacred Workday hasn't even started. To start working towards our Vision, we need to develop more concrete details on how we will do so; a blueprint if you will. Specifically, we will require a design for our Production System (how we deliver value to our customers) and our Management System (how we manage the delivery of value to our customers). In this chapter, we will first focus on the former.

## THE EIGHT WASTES

Why do so many businesses fail to deliver value to the customer? The Japanese have a word for it: *muda* or waste. You can easily find it throughout our Production System. Muda is all the activities that add no value according to the customer. In other words, the customer is not willing to pay for it.

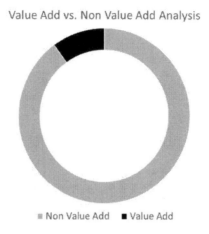

Value Add vs. Non Value Add Analysis

▨ Non Value Add   ▪ Value Add

**Figure 3.1** - In my 18 years as a Lean practitioner, value-add vs. non-value add analysis has revealed that a typical value stream has less than 10% value-add activity!

I have conducted value-add vs. non-value add analysis hundreds of times to discover that, typically, 90% or more activities used to deliver value to a customer are waste. In an eight-hour workday, this translates into **7.2 hours of waste!** A far cry from a Sacred Workday. And, for our customers, this turns into the frustration of having to wait.

But if a Sacred Workday is one where we *perform unifying rituals that embrace problems and transform them into continuous improvement, thus, restoring employee freshness and strength*, it is important we seek to understand this waste, rather than deny its existence.

Individually, the eight wastes are as follows:

- **Overproduction** is producing more than the required amount at the time and is the cause of all remaining wastes.
- By overproducing, **inventory** piles up.

- Inventory requires storage, and, thus, must be **transported**.
- When that inventory is required, those who need it are forced to **wait**.
- Inventory, not only hides **defects** but delays the correction of such errors.
- As a result, rather than send the defect back to the originator, we fix it ourselves or **over process**.
- By doing so, we create the need for additional **motion**.
- Ultimately, all the wastes lead to the most tragic waste of all: the waste of **human talent**.

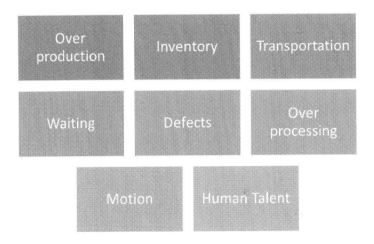

**Figure 3.2** - The eight wastes, often referred to as muda in the Lean community.

If you haven't taken the time to reflect on how you use your time at work, I encourage you to do so. You will be surprised at how much time you lose to muda.

Unfortunately, two additional factors impact our ability to have a Sacred Workday: *mura* and *mur*i.

## UNEVENNESS

Mura is unevenness in work, which typically manifests itself as employees working extremely hard for specific periods of time (the upper limit in the image below), followed by having little or nothing to do during other periods of time (the lower limit). This strain is a direct result of how the work is scheduled or unevenness in demand.

## OVERBURDEN

Muri causes employees to work at a harder or faster pace for extended periods of time. Overburden can also be caused by unevenness as the illustration below demonstrates.

The following scenarios illustrate the impact of muda, muri, and mura on a system and its employees.

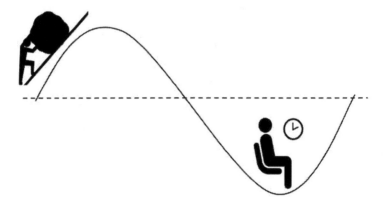

**Figure 3.3** - Mura or unevenness of work creates two adverse scenarios: 1) employees are overburdened when there is too much work demand or 2) employees are bored when there is not enough. With evenness of work, employees can work at a steady pace.

IMPACT OF MUDA, MURA, AND MURI

We need to process ten units of work in an hour, and it takes eleven minutes to prepare 1 unit if we follow the Standard Work correctly.

## Scenario 1

If we assign all these units to one employee, they must work almost twice as fast to complete the work. Per the Standard Work, it should take the employee 110 minutes to process the job, working at a steady pace. However, the employee only has one hour. Such strain would be an example of muri. When companies fail to understand their demand and capacity correctly, this situation occurs often.

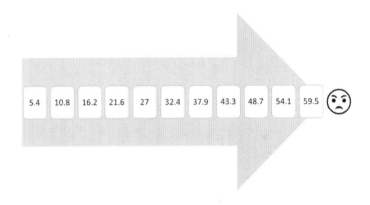

**Figure 3.4** - The employee must work at a pace 2x faster. In this example, the employees has to complete each unit in 5.4 minutes to meet customer expectations.

## Scenario 2

If we assign the same amount of work to this employee, but only assign two units in the first 30 minutes and the remaining 8 in the spare 30 minutes, this would be an example of mura, muda, and muri. In the first 30 minutes, the employee would have 8 minutes of additional time and would have to wait to receive more work, i.e., muda. In the remaining 30 minutes, they would have 120 minutes' worth of work and would not be able to complete it on time without working considerably faster, i.e., muri.

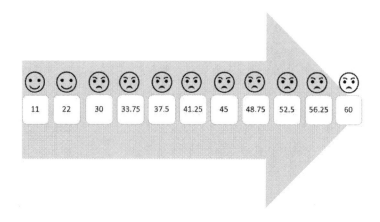

**Figure 3.5** - In scenario 2, we see the impact of unevenness of work.

## *Scenario 3*

The last scenario is the ideal one in which five units are assigned to one employee and the remaining five units to another employee, evenly throughout the hour. In this scenario, each employee has precisely enough time to complete their work with 5 minutes of spare time.

It would make common sense to go with scenario 3, yet so many companies struggle and fail to eliminate muda, muri, and mura.

Why?

The answer lies in our definition of a Sacred Workday: one where we *perform unifying rituals that embrace problems and transform them into continuous improvement, thus, restoring employee freshness and strength*. The key word in the definition is "embrace." To embrace something is to, not only accept it but to seek to understand it. Although most companies know that most of these wastes exist, they chose to ignore them. This turning of the cheek happens because either a) leadership feels these problems reflect them and lack the humility to accept their need to improve or b) administration personally does not know how to transform these problems into continuous improvement. We explored the former in chapter one. Now let's examine a tool that will enable us to take the first step towards the latter in our journey to create a Sacred Workday.

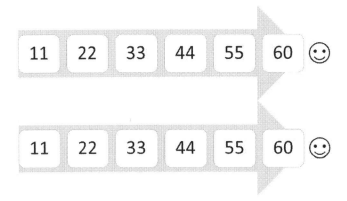

**Figure 3.6** - In the third scenario, work is evenly distributed to two employees throughout the hour. In this scenario, we can meet our customer demand at a pace which is comfortable for our employees.

## FRAMEWORK #1: VALUE STREAM MAPPING

John Shook and Mike Rother introduce us to a tool called Value Stream Mapping in a booked entitled, *Learning to See: Value Stream Mapping to Add Value and Eliminate Muda*. Although focused on a manufacturing example, it serves as a great tool to people if they can understand the principles and find ways of depicting what their value streams look like in their specific industries.

Shook and Rother define a value stream as:

*all the actions (both value added and non-value added)
currently required to bring a product through the main
flows essential to every product: (1) the production flow
from raw material into the arms of the customer, and (2)
the design flow from concept to launch.*[17]

If one can get past how technical the language is, there is a lot of
value in understanding what a value stream is. Let's use a real-life
example to understand the definition better.

## A TRIP TO THE DOCTOR

I recently moved, and my daughter needed a physical exam for her
new school. When I called a physician office, I was shocked that they
did not have any appointments available for two months! When I
finally found a physician who could see her sooner, we were made to
wait 40 minutes before seeing the doctor! From our point of view,
we define the value stream from the point we call into schedule our
appointment to the moment we see the doctor and pay for the exam.
In this example, my daughter is the "raw material" that flows
through the value stream and the "product" we were looking for is a
physical exam and, if required, any physician recommendations for
improved health.

It is important to note that materials, as mentioned above, can be
either physical, e.g., nuts or bolts, digital, e.g., a scanned insurance
application, or even human, e.g., a patient in need of a knee
replacement.

For those who can figure out what their widget is by striving
towards the principle of systemic thinking with creativity, Value
Stream Mapping is a powerful tool. For those who lack the
imagination, it will be frustrating and a waste of time. Lean, at the
tool level, is restricting and weak, whereas, Lean at the principle level
is adaptable and prevailing.

CREATING THE CURRENT STATE VALUE STREAM MAP

In *Learning to See: Value Stream Mapping to Add Value and Eliminate Muda,* the first step laid out is to understand what our product and service families are. To do so, just write down all the products and services that our business provides. Couple those that follow a similar flow from raw material into the arms of the customer together. Why does this matter? By managing and applying continuous improvement to one product and service, we can achieve and implement continuous improvement concepts for the entire family.

Once we do this, the next step is to develop the current state Value Stream Map. The point of this map is two-fold: 1) to form a realistic picture, i.e., grounded in fact, of the current state Value Stream Map and 2) to create consensus. The two most common failure modes in creating a current state Value Stream Map are 1) the map is assumptive and 2) there is a lack of consensus developed before shifting the focus towards the future state Value Stream Map. As a result, the current state Value Stream Map fails to deliver its intended purpose, which, ultimately, is to inform the future state Value Stream Map.

To create a proper current state Value Stream Map, depict the following elements:

- The customer and their current demand levels.
- Each process that the raw material goes through (a grouping of work done in flow without stoppage or inventory accumulation is a process).
- Data collection at each process, i.e., inventory, cycle time, value-add vs. non-value add and any other pertinent information.
- How material flows from the supplier of materials, from process-to-process and, ultimately, to the customer (typically, in a push fashion which promotes overproduction).
- How information flows, including any scheduling

(information is any knowledge required by a frontline employee to transform the material).

- A summary of your value stream, which typically shows lead time from start to finish and the amount of value-add time.

I won't go into any further specifics of how to Value Stream Map in this book as anyone can and should pick up a copy of *Learning to See: Value Stream Mapping to Add Value and Eliminate Muda.*

However, it is important to note that I have seen Lean practitioners become dogmatic about using the symbols used by Rother and Shook. They are tool-thinkers and will never know the feeling of transforming a business. Regardless of what symbols you use, the critical point is to elevate to the principle level and use the tool for its intended purpose.

It is also important to note that this map needs to be created by going to the place where the work happens or what is often referred to by the Japanese term, genba. A lot of people erroneously complete Value Stream Maps by having people from the value stream come into a room and draw a picture of what they think happens. Such an exercise is akin to misdiagnosing the root-cause of a problem and using that diagnosis to assign a remedy; the remedy is rendered useless. *How many times should we visit the genba?* As many times as required to get a realistic understanding of the value stream. I find it helpful to have a focus each time you go. For example, once we understand what our processes are, our next visit to the genba can be with a focus on data collection.

In chapter 1, we highlighted the importance of leaders using Humble Inquiry to build trust. This skill-set will be put to the test when Value Stream Mapping. Going to the work is about discovery and a genuine interest in learning more about the work. It is not a time to correct perceived errors or tell people how to work. This behavior will quickly amplify the fear culture and shoot down any effort to improve our business.

With a good grasp of the current state, and the muda, mura, and muri, we are ready to switch our focus to a future state blueprint of what our production needs to be to deliver value to our customers better.

The future state Value Stream Map is not a free-for-all; quite the opposite. Guiding principles, many of which, also guided us in defining our ideal rituals are used to create the map. It is important to note that these principles have been applied to production at Toyota and companies in other industries, spanning from health care to financial services, for several decades. They are **proven**.

## *Principle 1: Produce to Takt*

The first principle is to produce to *takt*. Takt loosely translates into a *measure*, *beat* or, even, *grace* in German. Delivering to takt means you can keep up with your customer demand.

The following is the equation for takt:

$$\text{Takt} = \frac{\text{Total Production Time}}{\text{Total Demand}}$$

When we can't keep up with takt, customers go elsewhere and find someone who can. Simple as that. Thus, it is essential to understand what our takt is to plan appropriately. As we noted above, failure to do so also results in more burden on our employees in the form of mura and muri. As the picture on the next page depicts, ideally, we want our employees to produce evenly despite what our demand levels do.

When planning to meet takt, it is essential to analyze the data we collect in our current state Value Stream Map to determine what our planned cycle time needs to be for each process. We use the value-add portion of cycle time for each process only and, through the process of continuous improvement, discover ways to eliminate the time associated with waste. Ideally, it should be 15% faster than our takt to account for unplanned events (the *shit happens* factor). However, if our planned cycle time is higher than our takt, then we will need to adjust our staffing appropriately. For example, if takt is 10 minutes, i.e., we need to produce a widget every 10 minutes to meet our customer demand, and our planned cycle time is 19 minutes, then we will need 2 employees to keep up with customer demand, i.e., 19 minutes ÷ 10 minutes = 1.9 (we round up in this case). Although some people are averse to math, we start to see how it is a necessary element in creating a Sacred Workday in which case we plan for our employees to work at a comfortable pace.

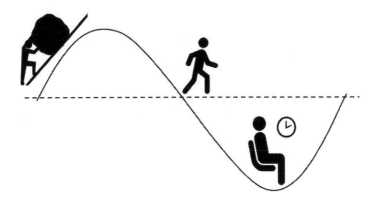

**Figure 3.7** - We want our employees to have a consistent production target to remove the burden and to deliver our products and services to our customers reliably.

## *Principle 2: Create Flow*

In chapter 2, we defined flow as the continuous delivery of value. This way of working is the most efficient, and every attempt should be made to achieve flow. As many of the following strategies should be applied to create flow.

## Simplify

It may seem obvious, but the first step in creating flow is to remove non-value add processes altogether. If they don't advance the work, get rid of them. Do this immediately!

## Co-Locate

Place workers together, whether it be physically or virtually using the right technology, in a way that work naturally flows. In today's virtual world, people are isolated and have lost the art of conversation. When people are physically separated, there is a lot of time lost trying to retrieve needed information with unnecessary back-and-forth communication. I worked at one client where glass separated co-workers. As a result, they would communicate with each other via office phone even though they could see each other and where an arm's length away. Sadly enough, it reminded me of a prison set up for visitation and their culture, at the time, was not too different.

## Cross-Train

It is typically better to upskill employees as down skilling or to teach someone a task beneath their skill level is not a motivator, i.e., the eighth waste of human talent. If you can upskill people and avoid hand-offs, you should consider it. Most of us have experienced the need for cross-training directly when calling a call center and being transferred to another department that can handle the question. If that employee were cross-trained to handle our issue and given the appropriate tools, not only would it yield value to us, but it would also enrich the employee with new skills and the satisfaction of being able to provide us value.

## *Autonomate*

This term translates into automation with the human touch.[18] At one company that I transformed, we automated our dispatch process by matching a claim review to the appropriate, available specialist. When the algorithm worked, it was more efficient and saved the dispatchers from having to do mundane work. However, when the algorithm couldn't find the appropriate, available specialist, senior dispatchers would problem solve, finding a comparable specialty or trying to negotiate with physicians to be open to take on the work. The latter scenario allowed them to exercise skills and, although the task was more challenging, it also was more rewarding. When you achieve a Sacred Workday, you go home feeling a right kind of exhaustion; the kind that restores your freshness and strength.

## *Synchronization*

In this scenario, employees work on the raw material in a synchronized fashion, each working on their independent part, but coordinated with each other. For example, in a physician's office, rather than have a physician exam a patient and take computer notes, you can have the physician exam the patient while a scribe takes the notes. This way of working requires that they synchronize and not trip over each other. The best example of this is the pit-crew in formula one racing.

## *Limit Work-in-Progress (WIP)*

The last strategy is to limit our work-in-progress (WIP) or inventory in-between two processes. The ideal limit is one, i.e., take one, pass one. Although we, most likely, will never achieve this ideal, it should always be the Vision. When we reach the WIP limit, production should stop to resolve any obstacles that impede flow. Restricting WIP is a psychological hurdle for many. They believe that by limiting WIP, they will be less productive. This outcome may occur in the short-term. However, what they fail to see is that, in overproducing, there is a cost as we previously explored in reviewing the eight wastes. Thus, when we limit WIP, in the long-term, we reduce lead time and are faster. This is yet another example of the Lean concept of *go slow to go fast*.

## Principle 3: Use a Supermarket Pull System to Store Inventory when Unable to Achieve Flow

There will be times when we cannot achieve flow due to various complications, i.e., unavoidable distances between work stations, drastic differences in cycle time, etc. In those scenarios, we will use what is known as a *supermarket pull system*. As the name implies, this is the creation of a storage area (be it physical or virtual) where we store materials until they are ready to be used. At Toyota, the use of what the Japanese call a *Kanban* (translated as signal card) is used to indicate a pull of materials and also to signal the production of more materials. As a result, the upstream process only produces what is needed, when it is needed, and waste is limited.

## Principle 4: Send the Schedule to the Pacemaker

Every value stream has a *pacemaker process* that dictates the pace of production for the value stream. As described by Rother and Shook, this process is typically the most downstream process that can be done in flow. Think of this process as the conductor of a symphony. The schedule should be sent to this process as it will determine the pace of the entire value stream.

## Principle 5: Level the Mix and Level the Load

This principle seeks to combat muri, mura, and muda. If you have various products and services that go through your value stream, it is essential to level them so that you don't have customers for one of those products and services waiting. For example, if we assume two products (product A and product B) have the same demand, and we produce them using the pattern AAAAAABBBBBB, then both customers of product A and product B will have to wait more than if the pattern ABABABABABAB were used. Through the use of forecasted demands patterns, we should determine the planned production pattern that achieves the appropriate mix. Again, we see that math is an enabler of a Sacred Workday.

In addition to leveling the mix, we should also seek to level the load by sending leveled increments of work to the pacemaker process. This strategy can be achieved using a *Load Leveling Box* (*Heijunka* in Japanese). Again, this can be physical or virtual. I have used this concept in a healthcare setting for discharging patients. When looking at discharge patterns, patients were typically released later in the week and also later in the day. This delay was a typical example of procrastination. By using a load leveling box, patients were scheduled for discharge in increments during the day, and we problem solved our way towards achieving this desired pattern.

## FRAMEWORK #2: TOYOTA KATA

We look to Mike Rother, yet again, to leverage another framework in creating a Sacred Workday. In 2009, Rother wrote a follow-up to Learning to See entitled, *Toyota Kata: Managing People for Improvement, Adaptiveness and Superior Results*.[19] In the book, Rother describes two *katas* (Japanese for routines): The *Improvement Kata* and the *Coaching Kata*. Let's use a practical example to understand this framework better.

### MOUNTAIN CLIMBING

In the image on the next page, we see two individuals who are attempting to reach the top of a smaller mountain; what Rother describes as the *Challenge*. You will notice that they also have a longer-term Challenge to achieve an even higher peak and a Vision of space exploration.

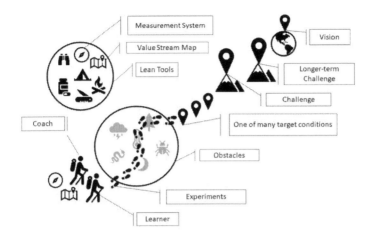

**Figure 3.8** - Both the Improvement and Coaching Katas are used in the example of mountain climbing.

One of the individuals has previously reached the Challenge in their previous experience, i.e., the *coach*. The other has not, i.e., the *learner*. For the learner, how to get to the top of the mountain is beyond what Rother refers to as their *knowledge threshold* and causes substantial discomfort. None-the-less, the learner presses forward because they have faith in their coach.

A good coach will provide the learner with a map that offers high-level direction on how to get to the top of the mountain (in our case, a future state Value Stream Map). This guidance shouldn't be confused with telling them exactly how to do it. The map shows various destinations along the way, i.e., *Target Conditions*, that the learner can aim for as they progress to the ultimate goal. But ultimately, the learner can decide what path within parameters of the map they want to take to get to the Challenge. In other words, they set the Target Condition. This Target Condition should cause slight discomfort but should feel attainable with the help of the coach. Once the learner sets the Target Condition, it is the coach's role to help guide the learner past the *obstacles* or *problems* through controlled experiments. A good coach will ensure the experiments don't cause the learner harm.  This care is accomplished using the Coaching Kata which consists of a series of five questions:

1.  What is the Target Condition?
2.  What is the Actual Condition?
3.  What are the obstacles? On which one do you want to focus?
4.  What is your next step? What do you expect to happen?
5.  When can I go and see what you've learned?

We will further explore this in chapter 5 on rituals.

Another critical tool we need is depicted as a compass in the drawing and represents a measurement system. It is crucial the learners understand where they are relative to the Target Condition. The learner achieves this understanding through observation at the genba and the gathering of metrics. Without this knowledge, the learner cannot determine their next step as they are ignorant of where they are.

In this model, the important thing is to experiment quickly. It is the only way to learn. It is vital that the coach create an atmosphere that allows the learner to feel safe and, thus, embrace problems and transform them into continuous improvement. Like the learner who is too afraid to take steps up the mountain, when we fail to take steps and experiment as a business, we will also metaphorically freeze to death and lose out to our competition.

Now that we have two dominant frameworks let's look at our organizational structure to understand where we need to apply them.

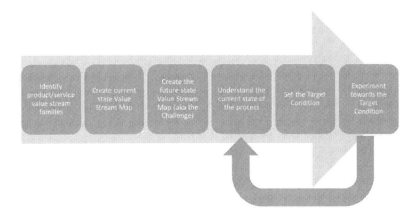

**Figure 3.9** - The following steps bring the two frameworks (Value Stream Mapping and Toyota Kata) together.

## LEAN ORGANIZATIONAL STRUCTURE

### LEVELS

It is crucial to implement the Production System and the kata methodology at each level of the organization. Thus, let's explore what each of those levels is and their primary focus.

In a business that achieves a Sacred Workday culture, there are, ideally, only **three levels** of hierarchy above the frontline employees. This management structure allows for a flat organization that can act agile like the reflex arc.

The top layer is the enterprise level and consists of the executive team. Their primary focus is to set the Vision and to make strategic decisions for the entire enterprise as discussed in chapter one. From a production perspective, it is essential they set the direction for how value streams within the organization coordinate with each other (the longer-term Challenge or higher mountain in our mounting climbing example above). We should apply this coordination to the following value streams: Market and Sell, Recruit, Hire and Onboard, and the actual value streams that deliver value to our customers, i.e., the *focus value stream.* What the picture of the mountain climbers does not depict is the role of the second coach. Executives play the second coach and focus on ensuring the coach follows the appropriate rituals to help guide the learner.

The next level down is the value stream level and consists of value stream managers. A value stream manager's primary job is to ensure value is being delivered to the customer. In typical organizations that manage in silos or vertically, this layer of the organization looks very different or doesn't even exist at all. But in a Sacred Workday culture, we manage the delivery of value horizontally. The value stream manager also serves as the coach in the coaching kata and guides various learners towards the value stream Challenge.

The next level down is the process level and consists of process managers. Within each value stream, we need to manage several processes at a more micro level. Process managers ensure their process is following the Standard Work for production that enables the value stream to succeed. As the learner, they are also responsible for improving the process they manage, continuously evolving to achieve new Target Conditions that lead to the Challenge.

There can be an additional layer of management between the value stream level and the process level, referred to as "the loop" level by Rother and Shook. This extra layer is necessary for larger value streams. However, I have found that it is not always needed and, in-and-of-itself, can represent waste.

Which brings us to the most critical level of any business: the frontline level which consists of frontline employees, also known as the value creators. The focus of frontline employees is to follow the Standard Work and deliver value to the customer. If they cannot do so, our business fails. As such, each level above the frontline level needs to focus on ensuring the frontline can deliver value to the customer. They do so by leveraging the Management System, which we will further explore in the next chapter, and by being coaches.

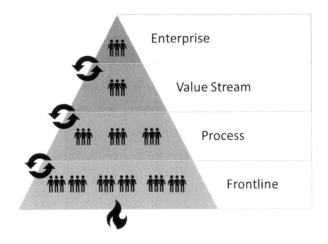

**Figure 3.10** - The different levels in a Lean organization.

As you may have observed, in an authentic Sacred Workday culture, everyone is a coach and a learner. Executives are not exempt and should seek a coach externally or internally if they find themselves without one. Frontline employees should do the same concerning the coach role, by attempting to coach peers who need help.

SPAN-OF-CONTROL

In my experience, effective coaching can only occur if there is a span-of-control for each manager of 1:6 (in other words, no one manager should have more than six employees reporting to them). Most organizations would consider this span-of-control to be unsustainable through a financial lens and would be tempted to increase the span of control. To them, the additional management is overhead. In a profane culture, they would be correct. However, in a Sacred Workday culture, this is not the case. When a manager properly coaches and develops their employees, they can increase the amount of value their employees can deliver to the customer. This improvement occurs because frontline employees expand their focus beyond *the delivery* of value to *improving* the delivery of value. A

Sacred Workday manager creates an army of problem solvers. Thus, they provide a return on investment on their salary.

## INTERLOCKING PRODUCTION SYSTEM

It is vital that each level have a Production System, and the Production Systems must interlock, i.e., the enterprise-level Production System locks with the value stream-level one, the value stream one with the process one, and the process one with the frontline one.

The Production System at the enterprise level, determined by the enterprise-level future state Value Stream Map, sets the direction for the Production System at the value stream level. The Production System at the value stream level, determined by the value stream-level future state Value Stream Map, must be designed with the intent of achieving the direction. This logic creates the interlock and trickles down to the frontline level.

In keeping this rigor, we ensure that the Shingo principle of *constancy of purpose* is achieved and that everyone is working towards the same Vision.

Now let's take a closer look at how to define the enterprise-level Production System blueprint.

# ENTERPRISE-LEVEL PRODUCTION SYSTEM

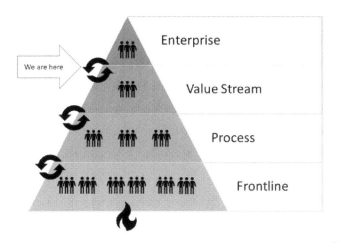

Although it is tempting to start our Value Stream Mapping efforts at the value stream level for a single product and service, we need to start at the enterprise level to create proper alignment.

Notably, once the focus value stream has been selected, it is vital to understand how the following support value streams will support it:

- Market and Sell
- Recruit, Hire, and Onboard
- Train

Without creating this blueprint for the Production System (the longer-term Challenge) that includes how all these value streams are expected to "talk," there will be limited improvements, at best, and complete chaos, at worst. It is for this very reason that so many attempts at achieving a Sacred Workday, ironically, makes things worse.

So why do so few organizations on their Lean journey start at the enterprise level? Here are some of the reasons:

- Leadership is not genuinely committed to achieving a Sacred

Workday.

- Leadership wants to start with a pilot at the value stream level to gain acceptance, i.e., curb their risk.
- Leadership is scared to role-model the new expected behaviors because they don't understand it.
- The organization lacks the guidance of a seasoned sensei.

But with commitment, courage, and the right sensei, this is the place to start that makes the most sense.

## ENTERPRISE-LEVEL CURRENT STATE VALUE STREAM MAP

Earlier in this chapter, we were introduced to the essential steps required to create a current state Value Stream Map. We apply these same steps at the enterprise level with a few modifications as seen in the diagram on the next page.

Individually, a enterprise-level current state Value Stream Map should display:

- The customer and current demand levels, i.e., a graph with month-over-month sales for the last year will do.
- Each value stream (in place of a process symbol) in the order of how material and information flows: 1) Market and Sell, 2) Recruit, Hire and Onboard, 3) Train, and 4) the focus value stream.
- Data collection for each value stream with a focus on outcome metrics, i.e., balanced scorecard metrics such as performance to speed, quality, and productivity. It is also essential to capture inventory waiting to be processed by each value stream, i.e., people, e.g., number of candidates that require training.
- How people flow from one value stream to another (typically, using a push system much after the need originates, resulting in a shortage of skilled employees).
- How information flows from the focus family value stream

to the support value streams

- To Market and Sell: with a focus on how to communicate capacity (typically not at all).
- To Recruit, Hire, and Onboard: with a focus on the staffing needs of the value stream.
- To Train: with a focus on how to communicate training needs.

- A summary, which should display the lead time from marketing to the delivery of value to the customer, segmenting out value-add, and non-value added time.

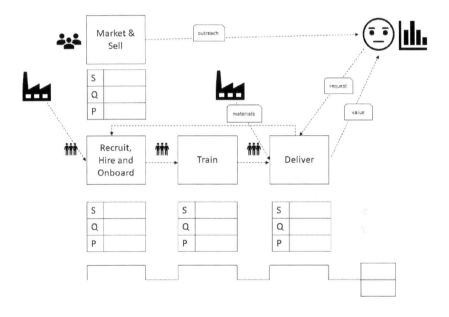

**Figure 3.11** - Sample enterprise-level current state Value Stream Map without data collection entered.

This enterprise-level Value Stream Map will often reveal some fundamental problems we need to embrace as opportunities:

1. Although production targets are given to the Marketing and Sales team, these targets are rarely communicated or shared

with the focus value stream. Conversely, the focus value stream rarely conveys (or even knows) its' capacity to the Marketing and Sales team. As a result, the Operations team is typically reactive as opposed to proactive when volumes spike. As such, operations cannot meet demand, and the customer is dissatisfied.

2. The first problem creates a need for more capacity, which we typically realize only after-the-fact. The remedy to this problem is usually the addition of more staff, placing added stress on the Recruiting, Hiring and Onboarding team that now has to compromise quality for speed.

3. More-often-than-not, the Training team is far removed from the day-to-day operations of what happens in the focus value stream and use ineffective methods that are removed from the genba and are not disciplined. As a result, employees are often poorly trained and require re-training (muda). Also, because of the second problem, candidates are typically rushed through training to get them into production, which makes things worse.

Because a Sacred Workday is one where we *perform unifying rituals that embrace problems and transform them into continuous improvement, thus, restoring employee freshness and strength*, these three problems now offer us the needed fuel to design a much more significant enterprise-level future state Value Stream Map.

ENTERPRISE-LEVEL FUTURE STATE VALUE STREAM MAP

The principles that guide our future state Value Stream Mapping outlined earlier in this chapter must also be applied at the enterprise level to ensure we accurately align our value streams and create our longer-term Challenge.

### Principle 1: Produce to Takt

In chapter 1 we defined ideal results, which included revenue targets.

It is essential to translate revenue into how many units of sales and production are required month-over-month. Simply put, if you have a sales target of $3M and, on average, each transaction is worth $200, then we know we need to sell 15,000 units for the year. This year-end goal can be broken down, month-by-month, with more aggressive targets towards the end of the year to account for increased capacity that a Sacred Workday will create. These targets will allow us to compute our monthly takt that will synchronize marketing and sales with operations.

## *Principle 2: Create Flow*

Let's recall our strategies for creating flow: simplify, co-locate, cross-train, autonomate, synchronization, and limit work-in-progress (WIP). Let's look at how to apply these at the enterprise level.

### *Flow Opportunity #1*

One of the problems in our current state is that training is too far removed from the day-to-day operations of what happens in the focus value stream and use ineffective methods. Rather than try and better coordinate these two groups, we will simplify, cross-train, and co-locate. Explicitly, we will remove the traditional training role, as is, and cross-train process managers on how to train at the genba using a proven training methodology known as *Training Within Industry* or *TWI*.

TWI has its origins in the United States in the 1940s. While our soldiers, mostly men, were fighting in WWII overseas, women were brought into the factories to build planes and tanks to help the war efforts. You may recall the famous image on the next page of Rosie-the-Riveter which became a trademark of the woman's empowerment movement.

**Figure 3.12** - Rosie-the-Riveter

In response to this demand, industry experts were brought together to come up with a way of training that would ramp up production quickly. The results were phenomenal[20]:

- 86% increased production by at least 25%
- 100% reduced training time by 25% or more
- 88% reduced labor-hours by over 25%
- 55% reduced scrap by at least 25%
- 100% reduced grievances by more than 25%

There are several reasons why TWI is more effective than the type of training most commonly used, i.e., show and tell.

The first reason is that the process managers work closely with the frontline employees to define how the work should be performed using a tool called *Job Instruction Breakdown* or *JIB*. This process of defining the work creates a sense of pride in the frontline workers. They feel honored and respected. We incorporate improvements into the JIB to ensure the latest version is always taught. When an external training department owns the training responsibility, there are two failure modes: 1) the improvements never reach the training team and, thus, they are using an outdated version of how to do the work;

or 2) there is a lag in the time it takes for the improvements to reach the training team and, thus, they need to retrain employees who were previously trained with outdated content.

The second reason that TWI is more useful is that process managers perform the training when needed at the place of work. There is no waiting for an external training department. If we recall the segment on span-of-control, this just-in-time training is enabled by the 1:6 ratio of process manager to frontline employees.

Lastly, when the process manager uses TWI, she takes ownership and is self-accountable for the success of frontline employees. In *The TWI Workbook: Essential Skills for Supervisors*, Patrick Graupp and Robert J. Wrona highlight how a process manager should train using *Job Instruction* or *JI*.[21] There is a TWI saying: *when the student hasn't learned, the teacher hasn't taught.* What this means is that when a frontline employee has not appropriately learned, rather than blame the employee, a process manager should reflect on whether they administered JI correctly. How refreshing is that? In this scenario, there is no external training group to blame.

## Flow Opportunity #2

The other opportunity for flow exists between process managers in the focus value stream and the Recruiting, Hiring, and Onboarding teams. Process managers also outsource recruiting, hiring, and onboarding responsibilities and are far removed from these processes as well. This creates a delay in hiring as there is too much back-and-forth between the two groups. In this scenario, a human resources team owns the hire, and the process manager is not accountable.

In this scenario, we will deploy the following strategies to create flow: cross-train, synchronize, and limit WIP. Specifically, process managers will be cross-trained on the Standard Work for the interviewing process, including the critical interviewing skills required; synchronization between human resources and process managers will occur so that concurrent processing can take place, e.g., panel interviews with a calibration session scheduled directly after; and a WIP limit will be implemented using a visual management tool called a *Kanban Board*, a derivative of the Kanban card we explored earlier, to create a steady stream of candidates and reduce lead time for hiring.

Both flow implementations mentioned above will reduce the lead time it takes to get employees hired and trained. However, in-and-of-themselves, they do not guarantee the focus value stream will not have to wait for skilled employees. To achieve that, we need to consider the use of a supermarket pull system.

### Principle 3: We use a supermarket pull system to store inventory when we cannot achieve flow.

In the 1950s, Toyota sent teams to the United States to learn more about mass-production. While on their visit, they found inspiration in visiting a supermarket named Piggly Wiggly.[22] Specifically, they were impressed with how the shelves in the supermarket were re-stocked and never seemed to run out of a product. Toyota translated this concept into manufacturing to ensure parts never ran out on the assembly line and called it a supermarket pull system. We now continue to evolve this concept and translate it into providing we never run out of skilled labor required to scale our business.

In our enterprise-level future state Value Stream Map, we will leverage two supermarkets: one in between the focus value stream and the Train one and the other in between the Train value stream and the Recruit, Hire, and Onboard one, as seen in the image on the next page.

If the ideal number of employees on each team, per our span-of-control target, is six, then we need to ensure our training supermarket has, at least, six fully trained employees ready to enter production at any given time. When six employees are pulled into the focus value stream, a Kanban signal is sent upstream to the training team to ensure we train six new employees. This activity, in turn, transmits a Kanban signal upstream to the human resources team to ensure we recruit, hire, and onboard six new employees so that we avoid a shortage.

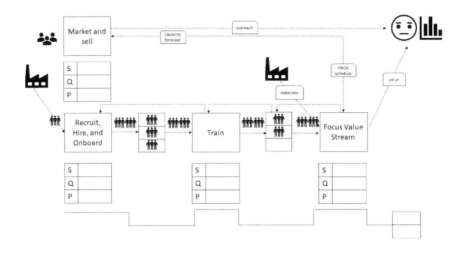

**Figure 3.13** - An enterprise-level future state Value Stream Map that includes two supermarkets that will ensure we never run out of skilled employees.

*Why don't more companies operate in this intelligent way?* One reason is that most companies don't understand their demand patterns and required capacity, i.e., they don't know the math (there is that necessary "evil" again) that enables this intelligent design. They are always running at a capacity deficit and placing an unnecessary burden on their employees. The other is that most companies are cost minded and not growth-minded (you can replace the word *cost* with *poor* and the word *growth* with *prosperity*). As a result, they don't hire and train employees for anticipated growth. The result is that they create muri for the existing employees, which worsens attrition and increases costs related to a) the process of replacing employees and b) paying more for overtime when production targets are not met.

It is important to note that in this model, growth comes in increments of a team's worth of production plus the improvements made to work by existing units. To minimize any downtime for newly skilled employees, ideally, the lead time to increase capacity by a full batch will equal the lead time to recruit, hire, onboard and train. To achieve the balance will require experimentation.

I also recommend that once we pull the team in the supermarket into production, they are managed by a promoted frontline employee, triggering the promotion of another frontline employee to lead the next team that we draw. It is essential this promoted process manager be involved in the recruiting, hiring, onboarding and training of that team. The bond of coach and learner is sacred, and we need to work on that as early as possible.

Lastly, it is important to highlight that new employees most likely will require additional floor space and machinery. Lean tools, such as 5S, create extra floor space and standardize what that space should look like, thus, making this easier to do.

In a marketplace where there is high demand for our product and service, the result of deploying the supermarket pull system is the ability to fuel high growth by scaling a skilled workforce quickly.

### Principle 4: Send the schedule to the Pacemaker

At the enterprise level, the pacemaker is the focus value stream. If this value stream cannot keep up with takt at the promised service levels, then additional sales or fully trained people will all be inventory (muda). The focus value stream acts as the conductor. At any point in time, if the focus value stream believes that its' capacity will not be able to support future sales' targets, then this communication needs to happen quickly. Slowing down our sales process to ensure we can keep our promises might create some discomfort in our customer base (and we might even lose some of them), but, in the long-term, we will please the customers we do serve, and growth will result. The rewards for those who are disciplined enough to sacrifice short-term gain for long-term success is that they will outlast their competition.

### Principle 5: Level the mix and Level load

Leveling the load and the mix is essential and removes stress from the focus value stream, allowing them to better achieve takt. To accomplish this, it is crucial marketing and sales also incorporate

Lean principles into how they operate, specifically: they need to be incented, not only to sell, but to sell the right mix of product and service. Like the focus value stream, they also need to produce to takt to level the load.

When marketing and sales concentrate on these two things, this translates into more steady demand for the focus value stream. In the absence of this, something known as the Bull-Whip Effect takes place.

**Figure 3.14** - The Bull-Whip Effect makes it difficult for employees to produce to takt and creates muri and muda.

After incorporating these five principles into our enterprise-level future state Value Stream Map, it is time to move on to the value stream level of our organization and design the blueprint, i.e., the Challenge, that will enable us to build our enterprise one. If our enterprise-level blueprint, the longer-term Challenge, is of our entire house, the value stream-level one may be for a series of rooms used for a particular purpose, i.e., the kitchen, pantry and dining room.

## VALUE STREAM-LEVEL PRODUCTION

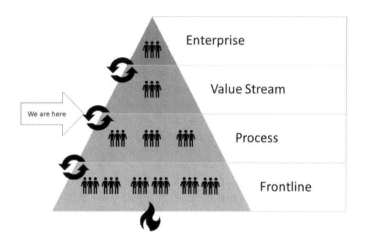

Now that we know the longer-term Challenge for the enterprise, it is vital for each of the value streams (both focus and support) to use Value Stream Mapping to define how they will do their part to achieve it. We recall, this process of the enterprise level cascading down the direction and the value stream level responding is known as Catch-Ball.

Each value stream should follow the standard steps in Value Stream Mapping. Although Rother and Shook recommend creating two maps, one for the current state and one for the future state, I recommend creating several future sates (plural). The first one should focus on *stabilization*, the second on *creating flow*, the third on *creating pull*, and the last one, on *leveling the load and mix* (you can combine this one and the previous one in some circumstances). Each one of these maps will guide the development of a series of Target Conditions leading their way to the value stream Challenge of achieving the aggregate benefit of all the maps.

We won't review how to Value Stream Map for the focus value stream as the steps highlighted by Rother and Shook in *Learning to See* can be followed. However, we will highlight some key things to consider when Value Stream Mapping for the support value streams.

## MARKET AND SELL VALUE STREAM

It is rare to come across a Marketing and Sales team that has done Value Stream Mapping. Marketing and sales teams often focus on one thing: the outcome of achieving a sale by any means necessary. What they typically neglect are the processes that lead to the sell, i.e., sending advertising materials, making phone calls, etc. When the value stream is mapped, it will reveal a funnel as seen below.

The best salespeople focus on the top of the funnel. Yes, they are tenacious and make more, consistent calls, i.e., they work to a takt. However, they also tend to perform certain rituals that embrace problems and transform them into continuous improvement. When a client hangs up in their face, they don't quit. Instead, they reflect and learn on how to refine their process next time they make a call.

The bottom line is that marketing and sales is a value stream. Talent and skills matter, but, in the absence of proven rituals, they are not sufficient. Value Stream Mapping is a significant first step to help standardize what those rituals need to be for all salespeople, not just a few, to succeed.

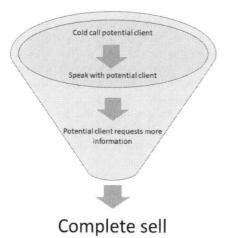

**Figure 3.15** - Sell funnel

## RECRUIT, HIRE AND ONBOARD VALUE STREAM

Like marketing and sales, it is rare that the recruiting, hiring and onboarding processes have gone through Value Stream Mapping. As highlighted earlier, this value stream has many obstacles. In my experience, the most prominent barrier is shortage caused by unevenness of how candidates move through the various processes of the value stream. A stressed human resources team is typically scrambling to fill roles. As they finalize the hires for critical functions, they usually neglect their funnel and, thus, lack a pipeline of candidates. Value Stream Mapping will visualize these obstacles and begin to create an awareness of the unevenness of how most businesses recruit, hire and onboard employees.

# PROCESS-LEVEL PRODUCTION

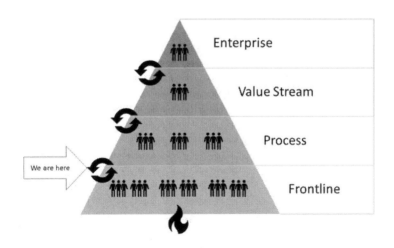

Now that we know where the value streams are going, it is crucial for each process within each of the value streams to create their response to create alignment further. It is important to note that this is the level where we will define how to do the actual work that delivers value to the customer.

## UNDERSTANDING THE PROCESS CURRENT STATE

As mentioned earlier, there is a Lean tool called Job Instruction Breakdown or JIB that can be used to help us understand the process current state.

As you see in the image below, the JIB focuses on identifying the operation or process, the parts, the tools, and materials, important steps (the what), key points that make or break the job (the how), and reasons for the key steps (the why).

No. _____

### JOB INSTRUCTION BREAKDOWN SHEET

Operation: _____

Parts: _____

Tools & Materials: _____

| IMPORTANT STEPS | KEY POINTS | REASONS |
|---|---|---|
| A logical segment of the operation when something happens to advance the work | Anything in a step that might –<br>1.  Make or break the job<br>2.  Injure the worker<br>3.  Make the work easier to do, i.e. 'knack', 'trick', special timing, bit of special information | Reasons for key points |
|  |  |  |
|  |  |  |
|  |  |  |

**Figure 3.16** - Job Instruction Breakdown Sheet template. Important steps (what), key points (how), and reasons (why).

The process manager should use the JIB to capture how various employees currently do the work on the team. The process manager should perform this activity at the genba through observation with minimum interruption to the frontline employee. If the frontline employee must be interrupted, it is important we remember to use Humble Inquiry to learn, rather than disrupt to correct or inject our bias. Remember, the point of this exercise is to capture what is; not to develop what the process should be.

In addition to filling out the JIB, the process manager should also capture cycle time and notate any defects observed. This data can be segmented by a frontline employee to help visualize those who have developed best practices. This analysis will come in handy when we are ready to apply continuous improvement.

For example, a frontline employee who has the fastest cycle time with the fewest number of defects, most likely, has developed best practices for the entire community. A frontline employee who is fast but generates a lot of errors probably has not.

When we compile all our observations, we typically see just how much variability exists. Although our frontline employees do the same work, they do it in very different ways. This variability is our enemy. If we are to achieve our purpose of sharing the rewards (financial and non-financial) that a Sacred Workday generates with our customers, we will need to work in a consistent, standard manner. The inability to do so creates a strain on those employees who are struggling while their peers have discovered better ways of doing the work. We embrace this variability as a problem and shift our focus towards continuous improvement.

## CREATING TARGET CONDITION #1

If we recall, the first Target Condition should focus on stabilization. Although this was defined at the value stream level on the future state Value Stream Map, we need to provide more details and flush out the Target Condition at the process level where there is more knowledge regarding the process.

### *Draft 1*

A small group of employees (two to three, at most, including the process manager) with best practices should be assembled at the genba to create the initial draft, using the JIB. This gathering is an opportunity to create the best-known way to do the work *now*. In the spirit of continuous improvement, we know that this is only a starting point and that good, most likely, will be better than what we currently have. The group should go through the JIB methodically, focusing on removing non-value add activities and incorporating as many best practices as possible. The team should also develop *Job-Aids* that will remove stress from the employees. A Job-Aid is a tool used to *help an employee perform a task more easily* (think about a codebook a grocery-store employee uses to look up the hundreds of bulk item codes).

An initial time-study should also be conducted to baseline how long it takes to perform the work, i.e., the cycle time. This number will be critical in helping us determine appropriate staffing levels to avoid muri.

## *Draft 2*

Once we complete the initial draft, we are ready to leverage another Lean tool: *5S (Sort, Set, Shine, Standardize, Sustain).* In short, 5S is Lean's version of *feng shuai.*

In the first S (Sort), we remove all parts, tools, and materials that are not used to do the work or create value for our customers. We store parts, tools, and materials that we use once-in-a-while. My rule-of-thumb is to throw it out, sell it or donate it if it hasn't been used in one month. The JIB proves to be useful in this scenario. People become emotional when it comes to getting rid of stuff in their workplace, even if that stuff adds no value. We should objectively use the JIB to determine whether things stay or go.

In the second S (Set), we should place all the remaining parts, tools and materials at point-of-use in a way that minimizes the wastes of motion and transportation. In doing so, we lessen the burden on employees. Also, designing a replenishment system – typically a two-bin Kanban – should be set up so that parts that require replenishment never run out.

In the third S (Shine), we define Standard Work on how to clean the work area. Many may overlook this step, but the more employees take pride in their workplace, the more sacred it becomes. Nothing says *I don't give a shit about where I work* like a messy workplace. I once worked at a hospital where a charge nurse assured me the Emergency Room was a sacred place, only to discover dried blood on the walls and dust everywhere.

In the 4th S (Standardize), we define Standard Work on how to perform the first 3 Ss. 5S is not a once-and-done exercise. It is a daily ritual that must be done to combat entropy.

Finally, in the 5th S (Sustain), the process manager should incorporate regular trips to the genba to ensure the first 4 Ss maintain their self-discipline. We will further explore the vehicle for doing so, *Leader Standard Work*, in chapter 4.

5S is critical in creating a Sacred Workday. If you stop to think about the places where you spend sacred time outside of work, i.e., your bedroom, your place of worship, your house, etc., they are well kept and clean (hopefully). There is a correlation between how sacred a site is and how well maintained it is.

## *Draft 3*

Once 5S has been completed, the employees should revisit the JIB and make any adjustments based on the newly designed workplace.

Once that is done, the process manager should conduct another time-study with the intent of demonstrating how 5S has impacted the ability to deliver value faster and with more ease. This timing will also serve as the target or planned cycle time for all employees to achieve. With this information, management can determine how many employees will be required once they are trained to do the work. With the above drafts completed, we can now create Standard Work for the process, which is the foundation for our Management System.

## CREATING TARGET CONDITION #2

Once a team achieves stability through experimentation, the next production Target Condition should focus on flow. This Target Condition requires cooperation amongst different processes in the value stream. The first Target Condition was all about cleaning up your own house first as they say. Again, although flow is defined in the future state Value Stream Map (the what), the how to achieve it is explained here where there is a deeper understanding of the processes involved.

Before creating the new Target Condition, we need to understand our Actual Condition (remember the use of the compass in the mountain climbing example). The JIB (and Job-Aids) should have been updated with each experiment towards stabilization to provide an accurate representation of how the work has transformed along the way. With this in hand, we should visit the genba to ensure the work is happening in accordance. We should also use our measurement system, with a focus on trend charts, to ensure stability has occurred. Once the current state is understood correctly, we can move on to creating the future state for flow.

### Cross-Train and/or Synchronize

With stabilization achieved, we should look for opportunities to cross-train and synchronize. To do so, we leverage the proven method of Job Instruction. As we do so, we need to remember the slogan, *if the student hasn't learned, the teacher hasn't taught.*

If we recall the eighth waste, we should always cross-train up. Even if cross-training down leads to a better process, it will demotivate people, and I would advise against it.

Synchronization takes a little bit more effort. For example, if we wanted to synchronize two processes (let's say process A and process B), then we would need to gather a small group of employees from each process. Each would bring a copy of their JIB. We would start with the critical step for one process, say A, and then ask ourselves if process B could perform their essential action at the same time or not. We would then meticulously repeat this for each critical step.

For example, with today's electronic, medical-record requirements, it's not uncommon to visit the doctor's office and have the doctor spend half of their time with you in front of a computer (you shouldn't have to pay for that!). At one of my previous clients, we created a Target Condition that would remedy this. Previously, the medical assistant would room the patient, the patient would wait, and the doctor would perform the exam, half of which, was spent typing. The planned cycle time for this was twenty minutes, which they achieved in the low teens. The Target Condition we established was to accomplish the twenty-minute planned cycle time ninety percent of the time through synchronization. When the medical assistant roomed the patient, the doctor was in the room reviewing their medical records. The medical assistant then exited the room, and the doctor began the exam. During the exam, the doctor would dictate critical parts of the exam out loud, and the scribe would record them on the computer. From the perspective of the customer, the exam went from fifty percent value-add to nearly 100% value add. At the time that I ended my engagement with the client, they were able to achieve timeliness in the eighties, which was an improvement of seventy percent.

### Co-Locate and Limit WIP

Once we cross-train employees and design synchronization, it is essential that we co-locate employees.

Co-location, not only makes sense from the standpoint of eliminating waste, but it also creates a sense of community. When employees work in teams and are together, they can support one another and help each other out when they are stressed. With that said, I find that it is essential we establish some norms when we co-locate, e.g., keeping voice volume at a certain level, etc.

WIP limits should also be put in place to ensure that inventory does not pile up. In an environment where we cross-train employees, synchronize, and co-locate, we should also slow down production when we reach the WIP limit. This unifying ritual allows employees to *embrace problems and transform them into continuous improvement, thus, restoring employee freshness and strength.*

### Autonomation

The last strategy to explore in creating flow is Autonomation. I encourage we autonomate after we stabilize and achieve flow without automation.

*Why?*

For the automate in autonomate to be done appropriately, you first need to capture the logic required, and we accomplish this using the JIB.

Autonomation makes some employees nervous. *Will I still have a job?* This worry is valid at profane companies that seek profit through gross cost-cutting methods. But at a company that aims to achieve a Sacred Workday, employees grow with the company. Autonomating boring, tedious jobs is a way of freeing up our employees to do things that are more mentally challenging and more fitting of their talents. As a result, their workday becomes sacred. When our employees go home, they feel like they used their brains. Yes, this is exhausting, but it is also a rewarding experience that restores their freshness and strength.

CREATING TARGET CONDITION #3

Once we achieve flow, we can establish our next Target Condition: to pull value (rather than push it) wherever we are not able to create flow.

The Target Condition for pull should include designing the following:

- a schedule that levels the load and mix
- sending the plan to one point in the value stream, the pace-maker
- how we pull materials to the pace-maker

Here is an example of a healthcare client that I coached to make it more real.

## *Leveling Load and Mix*

At the healthcare clinic, there were several kinds of visits:

- New patient
- Follow-up
- Follow-up with a drug screen

Only doctors (MDs) could perform new patient visits, and they took 40 minutes. Doctors could perform follow-ups, which only took 20 minutes. However, the clinic preferred that mid-level practitioners perform follow-ups so that doctors could see new patients and grow the practice. Follow-ups with a drug screen took 30 minutes but could be a lot longer depending on whether the patient had to use the restroom.

Our initial current state analysis of the scheduling process revealed several problems, which we embraced.

### Problem #1

Reception staff scheduled multiple follow-ups with drug screens during the same appointment slot, which created a lot of muri on the team. This practice also created a domino effect, as one appointment going over led to the subsequent visits going over as well.

With further analysis, we noted that there were about 15 drug screens, on average, per doctor. There were 24 appointment slots in a day. As a result, we created a Target Condition that receptionists could schedule no more than one follow-up with a drug screen per appointment slot. This new practice would be controlled by receptionists when checking out an appointment, as they would schedule follow up visits.

### Problem #2

Reception staff scheduled follow-ups with doctors, which didn't allow for new patient slots and which also resulted in light scheduling for the mid-levels.

Through the understanding of our current state, we developed a Target Condition that receptionists schedule all follow-ups with mid-levels first and program no more than 12 follow-ups with a doctor to allow for new patient slots to be available. Later on, one of the receptionists came up with a way to error-proof this by hard-programming the desired pattern of slots into the system – a feature they had never utilized – to enforce the Target Condition. This continuous improvement idea would enable the scheduling department that controlled new patient scheduling to find open slots more readily.

## *Send the Schedule to the Pace-Maker and Pulling*

Once we created the desired Target Condition for the schedule, we identified the pace-maker process as the exam process (we couldn't move faster than that process). Each provider had two designated exam rooms. When they were in one room finishing up with a patient, the other one would serve as a supermarket if, and only if, the provider went over with their other appointment. If they didn't go over, the team achieved single piece flow. Each provider had a dedicated medical assistant who received the master schedule, allowing them to be self-accountable to pull the patient into the supermarket.

Although I have already stated this before, the tools used to achieve these principles are not important. A pull signal can be a Kanban card if you are in manufacturing or can be a walkie-talkie if you are a nurse. What is important is the principle of *flow and pull value* and testing out different ideas, incorporating Lean tools where they make sense. The tool is not the outcome we are seeking. A Sacred Workday is greater than any one tool.

### CREATING TARGET CONDITION #N

After we achieve pull, if we still haven't met the Challenge, it is crucial to *seek perfection* and to continue to set new Target Conditions that inspire continuous improvement and close the gap. Once the sum of the Target Conditions achieved by each process equal the future state Value Stream Map, we are ready to define a new and improved future state Value Stream Map. Continuous improvement never stops. Growth never ends. The workday becomes more and more sacred.

As you can tell, this sort of mindset of excellence is very demanding. As such, we need a proven Management System to ensure we meet our high standard of production. That takes us to our next chapter.

# 3 | SUMMARY

- It is essential to establish a production blueprint that allows us to reach our Vision.
- Muda, muri, and mura are problems we need to embrace and transform into continuous improvement.
- Value Stream Mapping is a framework that allows us to better understand our muda, muri, and mura by visualizing it and creating a common language on how to discuss it.
- In creating a future state Value Stream Map, five critical Lean principles need to be applied:
    - Product to takt
    - Create flow
    - Use a supermarket pull when the process cannot achieve flow
    - Send the schedule to the pacemaker
    - Level both load and mix
- Toyota Kata is another framework that will help us design the Production System:
    - In the Toyota Kata, the future state Value Stream Map sets what we refer to as the Challenge (long term at the enterprise level and shorter term at the value stream level).
    - We set a series of Target Conditions at the process level, guided by the five Lean principles used in Value Stream Mapping, to achieve the Challenge.
    - There are two key relationships to understand in this model: the coach and the learner.
    - The coach guides the learner through the Improvement Kata steps using the Coaching Kata.
    - With a Target Condition in place, the focus becomes taking steps or experimenting to overcome problems.
- The key is to experiment quickly and learn.
- In a Sacred Workday, it is important to be nimble to respond like the reflex arc. Thus, there are only four levels of

hierarchy:
- Enterprise
- Value Stream
- Process
- Frontline Employee

- In this hierarchy, it is critical that each person be both a coach and a learner, ensuring Coaching and Development is consistent and happens from the enterprise level to the frontlines.
- To facilitate coaching, we maintain a manager/employee span-of-control of 1:6.
- Value Stream Mapping is often overlooked at the enterprise level but should begin there. In doing so, we create a future state for production that coordinates the focus value stream and the support value streams such as Market and Sell, Recruit, Hire and Onboard, and Train.
- Once we complete Value Stream Mapping at the enterprise level, the executive team communicates that map to the value stream level in the initiation of Catch-Ball. In response, the value stream level develops a future state Value Stream Map that allows the enterprise to achieve its' future state Value Stream Map, ensuring alignment.
- Once the Value Stream Mapping team completes the Value Stream Map at the value stream level, the process managers need to create a process-level blueprint using Lean tools such as a Job Instruction Breakdown and 5S to ensure alignment.
- There are several Target Conditions required to reach the desired future state Value Stream Map:
  - Target Condition #1: Stabilization
  - Target Condition #2: Flow
  - Target Condition #3: Pull and level load and mix
  - Target Condition #n: As necessary

# 3 | EXERCISE

- What forms of muda, muri, and mura exist in our company? How does this impact our ability to achieve a Sacred Workday?
- How does our focus value stream(s) interact with the support value streams? What are the problems that currently exist in how they "talk"?
- Do we currently have a long-term and short-term Challenge set? If so, what are they? If not, how does that impact our ability to know where we are going?
- What is our current organization structure? Does it support horizontal delivery of value to the customer? Does the span-of-control support the ability for a manager to act as a coach?
- Do managers act like coaches in our business? Is everyone given the opportunity to both coach and learn?
- Is worker variability an issue?
- What are the opportunities for standardization, flow and pull in our business?

# 4 | MANAGEMENT SYSTEM

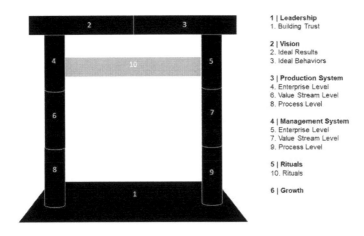

1 | Leadership
1. Building Trust

2 | Vision
2. Ideal Results
3. Ideal Behaviors

3 | Production System
4. Enterprise Level
6. Value Stream Level
8. Process Level

4 | Management System
5. Enterprise Level
7. Value Stream Level
9. Process Level

5 | Rituals
10. Rituals

6 | Growth

## FRAMEWORK: LEAN MANAGEMENT SYSTEM

Now that we have a blueprint for our Production System, it's time to do the same for our Management System. We looked to Rother and Shook to offer us guidance in creating our Production System. Now we look to David Mann and the tools provided in *Creating a Lean Culture: Tools to Sustain Lean Conversations* to do so for our *Management System*.[23]

According to Mann, there are three elements of a Lean Management System:

- Visual Management
- Accountability
- Discipline

In a Sacred Workday version, I have taken the liberty to adjust

Visual Management to Sensory Management as I have found that Visual Management is much too limiting and does not include auditory and tactile tools in its' scope.

Inspired by Jacko Willinck who wrote the book, *Discipline Equals Freedom*, I also added the word *self* in front of accountability and discipline.[24] As Jacko points out, the most reliable form of accountability and discipline is that which comes from the self, and that is what we should try and achieve with our Management System.

Also, we must add the critical element of Coaching and Development to the Management System. If we fail to give people aspirational challenges that tie to the Vision and fail to coach them towards those challenges, they will not grow, and we will not realize a Sacred Workday.

Most important of all, I have added Standard Work as the central element of the Management System. *Sensory Management, Self-Accountability, Self-Discipline* and *Coaching and Development* are all built upon Standard Work as the foundation, as we will shortly see. It is important to note that in this chapter we will discuss what the elements of the Management System are (the "infrastructure"), but we will not focus on how to build or use them as part of our unifying rituals quite yet. We will explore that in the next chapter on rituals.

Each of these elements must exist at the enterprise level, the value stream level, and the process level to create a Management System that produces a Sacred Workday; not just in one part of the organization, but in all. If one level is missing, especially at the enterprise level, we will not achieve the desired culture.

**Figure 4.1** - Five elements of our Management System (inspired by David Mann).

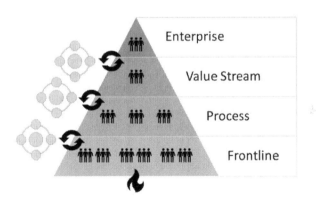

**Figure 4.2** - The Management System needs to be at every level of our business. Like the Production System, each level of the Management System interlocks with the level above and below it.

## ELEMENT #1: STANDARD WORK

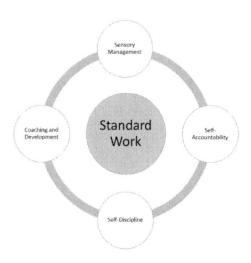

**Figure 4.3** - Standard Work is the foundation of the Management System.

Standard Work is a very misunderstood concept, even in the Lean community. There are few who I have come across who have demonstrated an understanding of it at the principle level. Most are stuck on thinking about Standard Work as an isolated tool.

When elevated to the principle level, Standard Work is only one tool in a system that seeks to create standardization to repeatedly and consistently deliver value to our customers. When employees do not meet the Standard Work, we *perform unifying rituals that embrace problems and transform them into continuous improvement, thus, restoring employee freshness and strength.* Without Standard Work, there is no baseline of what we expect to happen. Without an expectation of what should happen, there are no problems. Let that sink in for a minute.

Thus, Standard Work is the foundation of our Management System.

## Definition of Standard Work

Standard Work is the *current, best-known way to perform a process to yield the desired outcome.* It typically consists of five components:

- Required inputs to work on
- Steps and sequence of steps to transform the inputs
- Process characteristics, e.g., number of shifts, shift time, number of people, or anything else pertinent to how the employees should do the work
- Process metrics, e.g., planned cycle time and acceptable amounts of inventory or Standard Work-In-Progress (SWIP)
- Outcome metrics, e.g., # of units, quality

If these elements seem familiar, you are correct. These elements also make up the Target Condition. *So, what's the difference between a Target Condition and Standard Work?* In theory, there is none. Once a team achieves the Target Condition, a new Target Condition needs to be created to avoid entropy. This new Target Condition should be to maintain stability for a while, i.e., resting on our way up the mountain, before setting a more aggressive Target Condition. What is important to note is that even though a Target Condition's date is in the future, our employees need to try to achieve it immediately. This mindset is required to identify problems.

With that said, the only subtle difference between a Target Condition and Standard Work is that the former is Production System focused and the latter is Management System focused. In other words, Standard Work, in-and-of-itself, is a form of Sensory Management and should be displayed towards management, enabling them to detect when an abnormal condition exists. A Target Condition is what our frontline employees are trying to achieve in production.

We deploy Standard Work at the enterprise level, the value stream level, and the process level. The components don't change, only the lens from which the Standard Work is being observed using the Management System. For example, at the value stream level, our focus would be on the hand-off level, rather than the step-by-step level that we would see in a Job Instruction breakdown at the process level.

## ELEMENT #2: SENSORY MANAGEMENT

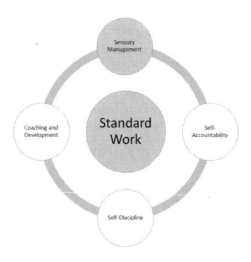

**Figure 4.4** - With Standard Work in place, we need to detect when the employees are unable to follow Standard Work, i.e., problems.

Although going to the genba is necessary, a leader does not have the luxury to do so all day. And when a leader does have time, where do they go and look? And what do they observe? Sensory Management helps with this dilemma by making it easy to detect 1) what the Standard Work is, 2) how we are performing to it, 3) what problems exist, 4) who is self-accountable for implementing counter-measures, 5) whether leaders are self-disciplined in ensuring the Management System is working, and 6) whether employees are being coached and developed.

## Definition of Sensory Management

We define Sensory Management as *sensory tools that allow the community to detect problems.* There could be thousands of forms of Sensory Management when we achieve a Sacred Workday, as there is a definite correlation between the amount of Sensory Management and how much a culture embraces problems.

## Real-World Example

Think of our business as a car. If we are driving to a relative's house for the holidays and the engine light goes on twenty miles into our fifty-mile drive, we have a problem (a gap of thirty miles to cover). The light is a form of Sensory Management that allows us to be alerted to a problem. At this point, we don't know what's wrong with the car; we know where we must go and look, i.e., visit the genba. If we chose to go on and ignore the Sensory Management, the problem could intensify, e.g., a flat tire could turn into a tailspin, leading to injury or even death.

Next, we lift the trunk and check out the engine. This act would be akin to visiting the value stream level in an organization. If we see black smoke, we may be able to narrow the problem down to the spark plugs, i.e., the process level.

Sensory Management is often viewed through the wrong lens and seen as policing employees, i.e., "big brother." But does the engine light judge how good of a job the driver is doing? No! If we have a license, we assume we have the skills to drive well. It is no different with our employees who should have been appropriately trained using Job Instruction. The light signals a problem with the system so that employees can *perform the unifying rituals that embrace problems and transform them into continuous improvement, thus, restoring freshness and strength.*

## Materials for Sensory Management

We will further explore examples of Sensory Management later in this chapter, studying them as we use them for Self-Accountability. However, let's quickly examine what kind of materials we should use for Sensory Management. Although this is tool-focused, I find that there is a direct correlation between the materials used and the level to which we achieve the desired rituals, i.e., principle-thinking. Specifically, the lower cost, lower technology solutions used to create Sensory Management typically result in higher compliance and higher quality concerning the ideal rituals.

### Visual Management

For visual management, my go-to is dry erase white-boards. The tendency is to jump to monitors that display digital information on spreadsheets. However, in doing so, the interactive nature of the board is lost, especially the element of Self-Accountability. When people draw information on a white-board by hand, they connect to the data. This style of learning is called kinesthetic learning.[25] When purchasing our dry erase white-boards, it is crucial to ensure they meet the following criteria:

- Can be placed in the production area.
- Are big enough for all employees to consume the information on them quickly.
- Are ergonomic and easy-to-use.

Given these considerations, I find that the best dry erase white-boards are typically on rollers. The rollers allow for mobility making it easy to transport them to create a flexible workspace that will evolve with each Target Condition reached.

## Audio and Tactile Management

For audio and tactile management, my go-to options are typical alarms that buzz and vibrate. There are plenty of them on the market, but my preference is for those that force the user to press a button or take some action to shut them off. Part of the Self-Discipline needs to be that until the right employee or team performs the correct operation, the alarm continues to draw attention to itself. I find that the most effective Standard Work also incorporates how the frontline employees should interact with the Management System, i.e., how to use and update Sensory Management as they perform tasks.

For example, at one of my previous clients, the Standard Work for our Huddle included shutting off the audio alarm that triggered the start of the Huddle once and only once the team gathered around the appropriate dry erase white-board we would use to guide the discussion. Compliance to this would ensure the alarm would retain its' value. Failure to do so would, not only render the signal useless, but would also create waste by adding yet another non-value add task for the employees to do. That would be very counter to a Sacred Workday culture we are trying to establish.

Audio and tactile tools are intended to drive Self-Discipline. When beginning our journey towards the creation of a Sacred Workday, this can be intense.

However, we should view these tools with the right mindset. These inanimate objects take the pressure off our employees to remember to take specific actions at certain times. Ideally, the audio or tactile alarm should go off before the action must take place. Audio and tactile tools assist workers in meeting their Standard Work. When they cannot perform these actions, the alarm serves as a reminder to reflect. Once employees establish the right mindset they will want more of these tools, not less.

As a best practice, whenever there are audio or tactile alarms that require action, I like to couple them with Visual Management to indicate whether employees took the appropriate action.

## *Managing to Exceptions*

Sensory Management is meant to signal a deviation from the Standard Work. As such, it is essential to think about how to signal when a problem exists.

If we use visual elements, we should only use two colors: black and red. Metrics that meet or exceed the target display in black, while those that do not display in red. I have seen visuals that use additional colors, e.g., green and yellow. This rainbow display is just a way of hiding problems and is indicative of a fear culture. The green color signals the need to counter-balance the red, whereas the yellow signals ambiguity in our understanding of how we expect to perform work. With two colors, the decision-making process is simple: you either need to speak about it or you don't. I highly discourage the use of more than two colors as it indicates leadership has not done the work to create the right mindset around the value of embracing problems.

ELEMENT #3: SELF-ACCOUNTABILITY

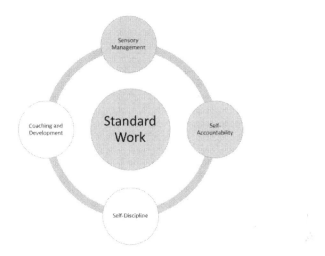

**Figure 4.5** - With Standard Work and Sensory Management, we need to create protected and structured time that allows our employees to be self-accountable to embracing and transforming problems into continuous improvement.

Have you ever tried to hold somebody accountable?

How did that go?

When it works, it's typically because the other person feels like they must do what you are asking of them or is fearful of your status, both of which, make the other person feel small. This dynamic is not as powerful as people being self-accountable.

Once Sensory Management is in place and the community can detect problems, we now need protected and structured time where we *perform unifying rituals that embrace problems and transform them into continuous improvement, thus, restoring employee freshness and strength.* This protected time is non-production time that, when used correctly, will have a return on investment.

Football teams create this time during games in the form of a *Huddle.* A Huddle is a small amount of time after each play where the team reflects on what happened on the previous play, adjust and plan for the next play.

The Huddle was invented in the 1890s by Paul Hubbard, a quarterback at Gallaudet, a deaf college in Washington, D.C. By forming a tight circle, him and his teammates were able to discuss plays without the other teams seeing what they were signing. [26]

At halftime and after the game, there is more time allotted to do the same activity but with a broader and deeper reflection, i.e., how the first half or the entire game went. Imagine what would happen if a team did not have this time to reflect? They wouldn't be able to adjust and would experience a high degree of frustration because of their low performance. So many businesses operate in this profane way, running play-after-play without stopping to reflect and adjust.

There is also another aspect of how football teams work that we need to translate into how we manage a business. In football, players are self-accountable to contribute to the team's success. When problems arise, Huddles allow them to put countermeasures in place quickly. However, if those countermeasures don't work, the coaching staff is responsible for problem-solving and making the appropriate adjustments. Like football, our frontline employees are responsible for playing the game or working the production line. When things are not going as expected and players cannot adjust on their own, coaches need to take ownership. This control doesn't mean that the frontline employees are not involved; quite the contrary. Coaches should solicit their ideas in a way that is conscious of their time and does not interrupt production. However, ultimately, management owns it.

In a Sacred Workday, the forms of protected and structured time for Self-Accountability are as follows:

- Planning Huddle (big plan)
- Intermediate Huddles (small check and adjust)
  - Unplanned (fast thinking)
  - Planned (fast thinking)

- Planned (slow thinking)
- Reflection Huddle (big check and adjust)

Let's explore these in more detail.

## Planning Huddle

Before the start of each shift, a team should conduct a Huddle for 15 minutes. Employees should be expected to arrive at work before production time to attend this Huddle. Initially, there may be some pushback, which is normal. But it is vital for leadership to remind everyone of the more extensive purpose and to make the connection of how the Huddle is one tool that enables us to achieve a Sacred Workday that gets us to that purpose. By starting the shift with such discipline, we get off on the right foot and, as a result, experience a much more relaxed and controlled shift.

The Planning Huddle has four key points that we should not compromise:

- It takes place standing up to reinforce brevity.
- It happens in front of Sensory Management, typically a visual board, to support a fact-based discussion.
- It follows an agenda (see below).
- The manager leads it, be it at the process, value stream, or enterprise level.

The Planning Huddle should have a simple agenda:

- What are our purpose, Vision, and Challenge?
- What is the Target Condition? (for the day)
- What is our plan to be successful?
    - Attendance
    - Assignments
    - Key communications

That's it! Using the football analogy, this translates into establishing what outcomes we want to achieve, what plays we are going to run to make it happen, and which players are going to play which roles. Although this agenda seems simple, it is not. Like most things in life, what appears simple requires a lot of foundational work to achieve. The ability to answer these questions involves a sufficient understanding of demand and capacity, which most teams lack. With a plan in place, the shift begins.

### Intermediate Huddles (Small Check and Adjust)

Once the manager sets the plan with the team, it is vital to check and adjust periodically throughout the shift. The goal should be to do so early and often. How fast would you want your reflex arch to work if your hand accidentally touched a hot plate? We should plan for this at specific intervals known as *pitches*. The need to convene will also occur organically as problems can and will happen at any time.

In the book, *Thinking, Fast and Slow*, Daniel Kahneman describes two types of thinking: system 1 and system 2.

System 2, according to Kahneman's framework, is our *slow, deliberate, analytical and consciously thoughtful mode*, whereas, system 1, is our *fast, automatic, intuitive and reptilian mode.*[27] We will use this framework to classify the different types of Intermediate Huddles we have.

### Unplanned (fast thinking)

Unplanned (fast thinking) occurs when employees encounter a problem in real-time and need to respond immediately, like our ancestors who used the reptilian mind for survival. These sorts of problems are not avoidable, i.e., employees are going to make the time for them regardless of whether a company is profane or sacred. However, in a profane work environment, there is a lack of structure, thus, increasing the time spent on such problems. This extra time can be critical. In healthcare, for example, their efficacy could be the difference between life and death. As such, it is essential we also have

Standard Work on how Unplanned (fast thinking) should occur. Luckily for us, such a standard already exists that we can leverage.

## *Andon*

In Lean, there is a form of Sensory Management, both audio and visual, that triggers this sort of Unplanned (fast thinking) called an *Andon* or signal light as seen in the picture below.[28]

When frontline employees encounter a problem, i.e., the Standard Work cannot be followed, they use the Andon to signal a problem to management. This act typically slows production. Now, it is the process manager's responsibility to help solve the problem with the frontline employee. The objective is to achieve flow, so that value to the customer is uninterrupted. There are also health benefits to employees when achieving flow.[29]

**Figure 4.6** - Sample Andon at Toyota.

If frontline employees cannot solve the problem, the Andon is triggered a second time, stopping the line. At this point, the rest of the team focus on resolving the problem. Depending on the issue, the value stream manager and other process managers may also get involved. Through the use of the Andon, we achieve three key benefits:

- It creates Standard Work on how to communicate a problem.
- It saves time by having management come to the problem, i.e., the genba, as opposed to the frontline hunting down management and wasting time.
- It keeps the frontline conscious of the Standard Work and creates self-accountability, i.e., where possible, the frontline employees should resolve the issue; where they cannot, the process manager should take ownership.

It is the frontline employee's responsibility to trigger the Andon when they cannot follow the Standard Work. By embracing problems at the point where they happen, we reinforce the Shingo principle of *quality at the source*. However, this requires the right mindset by frontline employees and that, as we know, requires the right mindset by management. When managers go to the genba it is essential they do so with Humble Inquiry and focus on the process. If they blame the frontline for problems, the frontline will discontinue the use of the Andon, and it will appear as if issues no longer exist. This scenario is a return to the profane.

Managers should take the frontline through the following series of questions, i.e., the Coaching Kata (with minor tweaks), highlighted in the previous chapter:

- What is the Target Condition? (for the current pitch)
- What is our Actual Condition?
  - What countermeasures did we put in place? (since we last ran a Huddle?)
  - What did we expect to happen?
  - What happened?
  - What did we learn?
- What problems are in our way?
- What countermeasure do we need to put in place?
  - Who will be self-accountable?
  - What do we expect to happen?
- By when will it be put in place? (this is optional as it is

redundant because the countermeasure should be immediate)

As you will see, each form of an Intermediate Huddle and the Reflection Huddle will utilize the Coaching Kata (with slight, appropriate variations) as the Standard Work. However, when dealing with fast thinking, the answer to question 5 must be, immediately, as there is an urgency to resolve the issue.

It is also important to capture information once the Andon is triggered. Employees typically record this information on a white-board near the Andon. Specifically, we want to create a Pareto analysis that captures each time the Andon is triggered and the type of problem encountered. This visual will aid us when we perform Planned (slow thinking). Also, the countermeasure and owner should be captured as well to create self-accountability.

> *But what if we trigger the Andon too often? Won't this slow us down?*
>
> Yes, that is the point. If the Andon is triggered, you are bringing problems to the surface, which is a good thing. In absence of the Andon, defects get pushed forward, resulting in rework or, worse, customer dissatisfaction.

## Planned (fast thinking)

At certain pitches during the day, it is critical that the team be able to go through the same unifying ritual as when the Andon is triggered:

- What is the Target Condition? (for the last pitch)
- What is our Actual Condition?
    - What countermeasures did we put in place?
    - What did we expect to happen?
    - What happened?

- What did we learn?
- What problems are in our way?
- What countermeasure do we need to put in place?
  - Who will be self-accountable?
  - What do we expect to happen?
- By when will it be put in place? (again, this is redundant as it should be put in place immediately)

This routine at each pitch may seem unnecessary given that we already have the Andon, but this isn't the case. A Sacred Workday is one where we *perform unifying rituals that embrace problems and transform them into continuous improvement, thus, restoring employee freshness and strength.* Therefore, we need to build these unifying rituals into our shift. The following Sensory Management tools will facilitate that ritual.

## Kanban Board

As previously discussed, a Kanban Board is a visual management tool that allows us to visualize our inventory or work-in-progress (WIP). There are plenty of digital versions of this tool on the market, but again, I recommend using a white-board and sticky-notes to reinforce the ritual. On a Kanban Board, physical representations of our WIP in the form of sticky-notes move through a series of lanes that represent processes. In higher volume areas, we can replace a physical representation with a count. Kanban Boards typically have WIP limits. When we reach these, employees are forced to stop upstream production and resolve problems at the bottle-neck process so that we can create flow. In doing so, we improve lead time. By visualizing the inventory and understanding the issues that get in the way of progress, employees can self-adjust and act like the reflex arc.

## Hour-by-Hour Board

An Hour-by-Hour Board is a visual management tool that is used to track how teams are performing to takt on an hourly pitch (depending on the process, the pitch can be appropriately adjusted). At each pitch, team members update their board with how much they produced to target. They also capture problems that are getting in their way (see Pareto analysis above in Andon section). Like the Andon, team members should also capture countermeasures and owners to create self-accountability.

When teams are not on pace to meet takt, one countermeasure that teams can put in place is to self-adjust their pace and work faster (a short-term countermeasure, which also creates muri). I have found Hour-by-Hour Boards to be very powerful. Most of the time, the most significant problem in the way of producing evenly is awareness of takt. In that case, having Sensory Management, in-and-of-itself, acts as the countermeasure, creating the needed knowledge for employees to work at an even pace.

### Kamishibai Board

A *Kamishibai Board* (also referred to as a Task Board) is another tool used to check and adjust. Tasks that teams need to accomplish are identified using cards that are red on one side and traditionally green on the other (although I recommend replacing the green with white: see the Managing to Exceptions section above to recall the why). The default is to have the card in the red position. When teams complete a task, the card is turned over to the white side. This visual is used to ensure critical tasks are completed in a timely fashion and are not forgotten; ultimately, allowing for self-accountability by team members.

### Planned (slow thinking)

Planned (slow thinking) allows for more deliberate, slow problem-solving. There are many methodologies for problem-solving out there, e.g., the eight steps, etc., but, I find it helpful to use the same approach regardless of our problem-solving situation, i.e., planned, unplanned, fast thinking, slow thinking. This consistency in methodology creates clarity and simplicity for all employees. As such, once again, we use the Coaching Kata questions:

- What is the Target Condition?
- What is the Actual Condition?
  - What countermeasures did we put in place? (since we last met)
  - What did we expect to happen?
  - What happened?
  - What did we learn?
- What problems exist? Which one is the focus?
- What is the next step? What do we expect to happen?
- When can I go and see what you learned?

If we recall, this ritual takes place between the coach and the learner in front of what we will call a *PDCA (Plan Do Check Adjust) Board.* This ritual should take place at the process level where the learner is the process manager, the coach is the value stream manager, and the second coach is an executive. Frontline staff, although not always directly involved, should be kept informed of what the learner is working on and the learner should consistently seek their input during Huddles. This ritual should also happen at the value stream level where the learner is the value stream manager, the coach is an executive, and the second coach is another executive.

Management already created the Challenge and the Target Condition in our Production System design. By beginning our problem solving with a review of these, we ensure there is alignment on where we are trying to go, i.e., a point along the path towards the top of the mountain.

To understand our Actual Condition, we can leverage our Sensory Management along with going to the genba to see for ourselves. Doing so gives us a realistic understanding of where we currently are relative to where we want to be. Going to the genba also enables us to see what our problems are via direct observation. A helpful Lean tool to use is *5-why analysis* where, in theory, we ask *why* until we get to the root-cause of the problem. Practically, 5-why can be exasperating and turn people off. Therefore, I recommend it be used more as a mindset while using Humble Inquiry to get to the root-cause.

Once we know the root-cause, we are ready to plan an experiment (the P in PDCA) specifically designed to overcome that one problem. This experiment should be executed by the frontline staff in production to see if it moves us forward towards our Target Condition. This participation reinforces what I stated on the previous page regarding keeping the frontline staff engaged in what the learner is doing.

Because a Target Condition is beyond our knowledge threshold, it should take several experiments to overcome a problem. Through reflection and learning, we will overcome a problem and then move onto the next one, so-on-and-so-forth, until we finally meet our Target Condition. The key is to fail fast and learn.

Once we have reached our Target Condition, it is essential to translate what we learned into our Production System and Management System. For example, the process manager should update the Job Instruction Breakdown on the Production System side, and the Standard Work on the Management System side.

Most importantly, it is essential for teams to celebrate once they have reached a Target Condition as it is the materialization of us *performing unifying rituals that embrace problems and transforming them into continuous improvement, thus, restoring employee freshness and strength.* At this point, our next Target Condition should be to sustain our Actual Condition. If we were mountain climbing and reached a milestone on the map, we would stop and get some rest. However, we wouldn't want to wait too long because this could put us at risk from external factors. This same thinking applies to business.

### Reflection Huddle (Big Check and Adjust)

At the end of the shift, there should also be a Huddle that focuses on reflection, and that makes any appropriate adjustments for the next shift. The same critical points for a Planning Huddle, i.e., standing, in front of Sensory Management, using an agenda, and led by the manager should be followed. The only thing that requires modification is the agenda, which should be as follows:

- What is the Target Condition? (for the shift)
- What is our Actual Condition?
    - What countermeasures did we put in place?
    - What did we expect to happen?
    - What happened?
    - What did we learn?
- What problems got in our way?
- What additional countermeasures will we put in place?
    - Who will be self-accountable?
    - What do we expect to happen?
- By when will they be put in place?
- Is there anyone we should recognize? (added)

From a psychological point of view, this Huddle is very important. When employees reflect on their shift and feel a sense of accomplishment and advancement, the work day is transformed and made sacred. Without this reflection, employees feel like they did a *bunch of stuff*. Even if we don't succeed, learning about why we didn't and adjusting, in-and-of-itself, is a form of success.

ELEMENT #4: SELF-DISCIPLINE

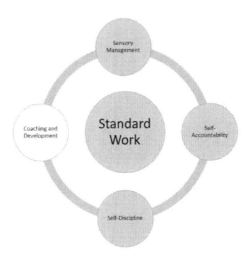

**Figure 4.7** – Self-Discipline ensures we define and maintain Standard Work, make problems detectable, and transform them into continuous improvement.

Let's recall our definition of a Sacred Workday: one where we *perform unifying rituals that embrace problems and transform them into continuous improvement, thus, restoring employee freshness and strength*. Each part of our Management System plays a role in operationalizing this definition so that it becomes our reality. Standard Work provides a baseline from which we can define problems. Sensory Management makes problems detectable. Self-Accountability creates protected and structured time where we *perform unifying rituals that embrace problems and transform them into continuous improvement, thus, restoring employee freshness and strength*. Now we turn to Self-Discipline to ensure this happens consistently. This element of the Management System works on securing Self-Discipline is in place around all the other parts. It seeks to answer the following questions:

- Are we disciplined about defining and maintaining Standard Work?

- Are we disciplined about ensuring our Sensory Management makes problems detectable?
- Are we disciplined about transforming our problems into continuous improvement through Self-Accountability?

## *Self-Discipline Begins with Time Management*

If you recall, in chapter 3, we introduced the concept of value-add vs. non-value add to better understand our production. We can also apply this concept to better understand our time. Management, in a profane organization, spends most of their time in conference rooms, removed from the genba. Much of this time is waste.

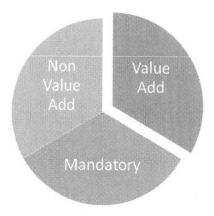

**Figure 4.8** - The concept of value-add vs. non-value add can also be applied to the most sacred thing of all: our time.

However, in a Sacred Workday culture, time is spent at the genba as planned using *Leader Standard Work*. Specifically, Leader Standard Work is *standardized, and protected time for us to perform the unifying rituals that embrace problems and transform them into continuous improvement, thus, restoring employee freshness and strength.*

At each level, Leader Standard Work seeks to ensure:

- The person performing Leader Standard Work, at their level:

- Develops and maintains Standard Work
- Keeps Sensory Management up-to-date
- Is Self-Accountability and responsive to escalations
- Coaches and develops employees
- At the levels below, goes to the genba to ensure:
  - Standard Work is developed and maintained
  - Sensory Management is up-to-date
  - Self-Accountability is happening
  - Coaching and Development of employees is occurring
  - Self-Discipline (Leader Standard Work) is followed

The diagram below shows how much time should be standardized and protected for the Management System at each level of the organization.

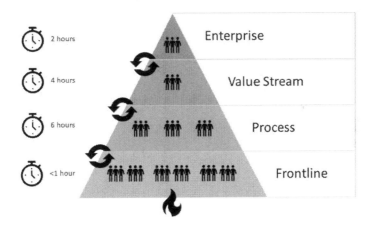

**Figure 4.9** - At each level of the organization, Leader Standard Work provides the necessary Self-Discipline to ensure the Management System is working as intended.

## Genba

Once we protect our time, we need to use that time to better understand how our business is performing. This comprehension won't happen at your desk; it occurs at the genba. It is critical that when going to the genba, Humble Inquiry is the modus operandum. With it, the visit will yield tremendous results. Without it, the effect will be disastrous. Management should also use the same Coaching Kata questions when going to the genba to be consistent:

- What is the Target Condition? (We can apply these questions to a process, Sensory Management, Self-Accountability, Coaching and Development, or Self-Discipline, depending on what your focus is for that visit)
- What is the Actual Condition?
  - What countermeasures did we put in place?
  - What did we expect to happen?
  - What happened?
  - What did we learn?
- What problems exist? Which one is the focus?
- What is the next step? What do we expect to happen?
- When can I go and see what you learned?

Remember, a leader should offer help if-and-only-if the person they are coaching has exhausted their experimentation and is genuinely at a stand-still. Before that, the leader's form of support is to go through the routine at the genba, getting the person they are coaching to **think**.

Before engaging in dialogue with the manager for the area you are visiting, I like to see how many of these questions I can answer directly by looking at their Sensory Management. If I can't answer them, then that is probably a right place to focus our discussion.

## ELEMENT #5: COACHING AND DEVELOPMENT

**Figure 4.10** – Coaching and Development ensures employs grow so that our business can grow.

The last element of our Management System is one of the most important ones: *Coaching and Development.* Our business is our people, so if our company is going to grow, our people need to grow; plain and simple. This personal growth won't just happen organically. Leadership needs to engineer it. The, appropriately named, GROW Model provides a structured approach we can follow.[30]

## *GROW Model*

GROW standards for:

- Goal
- Reality
- Obstacles / Options and
- Way Forward

## *Goal*

The first step in the model is to ensure employees have a goal. For a manager to coach, it is crucial they clarify what the goal is for their employee's "position" and how that role aligns to the Target Condition, Challenge, and, ultimately, the Vision of the company. The primary tool used to accomplish this is a development plan.

### *Development Plan*

A development plan builds upon and mimics some aspects of Standard Work:

- Outcome metrics (community success)
- Process metrics (personal success that enables community success)
- Process characteristics (the way in which an employee does the work)
- Ideal rituals (how employees behave)

It is essential that the outcome metrics for the company, value stream, and process team be listed first. Creating a Sacred Workday culture is also building a team culture where the *I* takes a back seat to our purpose as a whole, which focuses on our customer and our employees as a collective community. Thus, there is no such thing as individual success without team success.

There are two ways everyone can contribute to the success of the team.

The first way is by following the Standard Work (the first three bullets above), be it for the process at the frontline level or the management of the process at the management level, i.e., Leader Standard Work. In doing so, employees honor the collective knowledge that has developed the Standard Work and allow for a baseline of continuous improvement. Whenever we miss the mark at achieving our outcome metrics and process metrics, we should also question whether employees are adhering or attempting to subscribe to Standard Work. If they are not, then that must be addressed, as we have no way of knowing whether the Standard Work is sufficient if employees do not follow it. If they are, then we know the process manager must lead the improvement of Standard Work as it is deficient.

The second way employees can contribute to the success of the team is based on how they behave. Remember, we want ideal results and ideal rituals. Employees should demonstrate behavior that is consistent with what leadership defined in our Vision. For example, for the Shingo principle of *focus on the process*, we may identify the following as a desired ritual: employees come to team Huddles with problems that are preventing them from performing the Standard Work. We can observe and record this behavior. It also demonstrates the principle because employees will only achieve this ritual if they trust that there is a no blame work environment. In a Sacred Workday culture, not only are employees expected to deliver value, but they are also expected to *perform unifying rituals that embrace problems and turn them into continuous improvement, thus, restoring employee freshness and strength*. As such, we create an army of problems solvers that will render our competition helpless.

It is essential a manager share the development plan with each of their direct reports to ensure there is clarity. The development plan is not a negotiation. It is the manager's responsibility as the coach to set the goal. An employee, as the learner, can add elements to the development plan that align to the goal. However, the employee cannot subtract anything.

### Weighting

I find that it is essential to place an equal weighting on all the elements of a development plan or risk sending the wrong message. We are striving for ideal results **and** ideal rituals. One is not more or less important than the other. However, I do find that if we focus on the ideal rituals, we will achieve the ideal results.

## Reality and Obstacles

Once the manager establishes the goal, it is critical the manager understand the reality of where their direct reports are relative to the said goal. With tools already mentioned in previous chapters, i.e., Sensory Management, Humble Inquiry, and Self-Discipline with a focus on going to the genba, the manager should be able to do so quickly without bias. Coaching and Development will only be as good as the quality of visits to the genba. Paying a visit to where the work happens is the fuel for proper Coaching and Development. Imagine a baseball coach who wasn't in the dugout watching the game and observing his players? He would be useless as a coach. So are managers who don't observe their employees.

## Options and Way Forward

Not all employees are the same. It is vital for us to realize this and adapt our coaching style accordingly to determine options and a way forward. The *Skill/Will Matrix* as seen on the next page is one tool that helps a manager do so.

As the picture shows, the higher the will and the skill, the more options, and autonomy a manager should provide to an employee. When an employee has lower will and skill, the manager should give him fewer options and more direction. Employees who lack will but have skill need to be inspired. It could be that they are bored because their manager is not challenging them appropriately and a manager should self-reflect to see if this is the case.

And, lastly, employees with a high will but low skill need training using our proven method of Job Instruction. The goal is always to move as many employees as we can into the high skill, high will quadrant. When employees move into this quadrant, we start to become the reflex arc, and executive leadership can be freed up to focus on external factors and strategy. However, it is also important to remember that the quadrants employees fall into are not static. For example, by limiting options to a high skill, high will employee, you may influence them to become low will quickly. Thus, it's important to be aware of where an employee is in this matrix continuously.

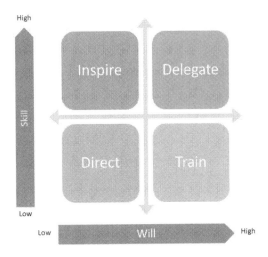

**Figure 4.11** - The Skill/Will Matrix is a tool that allows us to adapt our coaching style depending on which quadrant the learner resides.

ONE-ON-ONE COACHING AND FEEDBACK

Unlike most organizations, a Sacred Workday organization does not provide feedback twice a year at a mid and annual review. How much sense does it make to give people only two opportunities to reflect and adjust? We also provide it during those times, but, also, offer it during monthly one-on-one coaching sessions and as needed through our daily interactions with employees using the Management System. The Shingo principles of *respect for the individual* means giving employees feedback early and often regarding the reality of where they stand in comparison to their goal. By providing feedback to employees, we also make them aware of problems they may not be aware exist. However, feedback is not easy to give. In the book, *Thanks for the Feedback: The Science and Art of Receiving Feedback Well,* the authors, Douglas Stone and Sheila Heen, provide us with insight into why. According to them, receiving feedback implies we are not good enough as we are.[31] As a result, it is essential we intelligently deliver feedback.

## FEEDBACK MODEL

The *Feedback Model* as seen on the next page is one that I have found highly useful.

The first step is critical: ensuring the employee is ready to receive feedback. We need to ensure the employee receiving the feedback is not distracted, has the time, and is in the right emotional state to receive the input. This criterion is more straightforward to meet when a one-on-one is scheduled. However, for ad-hoc feedback, this could be a bit trickier. Although I am a fan of a transparent and open work environment, I always suggest finding a private place to provide feedback that might not be well-received.

Next, it is crucial to provide fact-based observation. Remove bias or emotion from what you share with the person. This objectivity will increase the likelihood they will receive the feedback.

It is also a good idea for the person providing the feedback to tie back how their observation impacts the broader community. For example, if an employee is habitually late to work, you may want to mention how this puts stress on the team, causing them to work overtime and miss sacred time with their families.

The next step is always the most difficult, especially if you are a talker. At this point, it is essential to pause and listen. If the recipient doesn't react, this is an excellent point in time to practice Humble Inquiry. In the above example regarding tardiness, we could ask the following question with sincerity: *what are the problems impacting your ability to get to work on time?* If done effectively, and if the trust has already been built prior, the employee will open and share some of their obstacles.

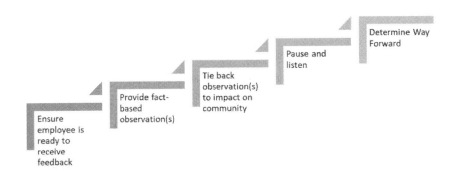

**Figure 4.12** - Standard Work for giving feedback gives everyone a routine to follow to refine this challenging skill to master.

Lastly, we want to determine a way forward. Depending on where an employee falls on the Skill/Will Matrix, you may want to offer more freedom and variety of choices or less.

At any point in time, it is essential to use the Feedback Model for both positive and constructive feedback. People like to hear what they do well, and managers should reinforce any positive behavior.

It is essential the manager document an employee's progress towards their goal along the way. Again, I find that a low-tech solution works well: simple templates in Microsoft Word that a manager can print out, write on, and store in employee-specific folders. I find that using physical templates, as opposed to digital ones, creates more intimacy during the one-on-one coaching session. Have you ever been to the doctor's office only to find yourself speaking to a doctor who is typing notes on a computer, rather than paying attention to you? Doesn't feel too personal, does it?

PERFORMANCE RATING

As much as a performance rating may scare employees, especially in smaller businesses that may never have taken employees through this process, it is essential we measure how our employees perform to help them grow. Remember, it is the ultimate sign of respect to let employees know where they stand early and often and to coach them to improve. With the right coaching and developing, the performance rating should not feel punitive, but instead, be viewed as a tool for continuous personal improvement. It is also important to note that an employee's performance rating is a direct representation of their manager's ability to coach and develop them. With that said, I find the following performance rating system to be useful:

- 1 – Below standard and not continuously improving
- 2 – Below standard and continually improving
- 3 – At standard
- 4 – Exceeding standard

The criteria for what it means to meet standard should be apparent and spelled out in the development plan. In a Sacred Workday culture there is no ambiguity, and when there is, we clarify.

## PAY-FOR-PERFORMANCE

As we noted in chapter 2, part of our purpose is to share the rewards (financial and non-financial) that a Sacred Workday generates with our employees and customers. There are two elements of pay-for-performance that we need to address: 1) base salary and 2) bonuses. Of course, all raises, and bonuses should be contingent upon the business being profitable, but if we follow the formula in this book, this will not be an issue.

### Base Salary

Periodically or when significant continuous improvement takes place, a company should re-assess the market rate for each role in the company. This analysis is essential to do because, in a Sacred Workday culture, employees *perform unifying rituals that embrace problems and transform them into continuous improvement, thus, restoring employee freshness and strength*. Thus, roles continuously evolve to provide more and more value.

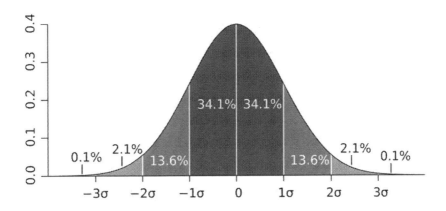

**Figure 4.13** - A standard deviation of the market rate for a specific role.

Let's say the image above represents the normal distribution curve where the mean is the average salary for a specific role in the marketplace. When first hiring an employee into our business, the company should pay them at the average. Some companies hire and pay below the average with the logic that employees must work their way towards the average. However, if you are hiring the right people by doing your due diligence, you should pay them what they are worth. If you don't, somebody else will. At an employee's yearly review, employees who exceed the standard should be bumped up in salary anywhere from 1 to 2 standard deviations. The only exception is if they are promoted, at which point, they should be bumped up to the average for their new position (still a raise).

Employees meeting the standard should be bumped up within one standard deviation of the norm. Some may say this doesn't make sense.

*Why should people be given a raise just for meeting the standard?*

In a Sacred Workday culture where we continuously raise targets, and the company is ever growing, meeting the standard has significance as it ensures growth. Employees should share in the benefits of that growth.

The next two categories are a bit tricky.

Employees who are below the standard and continuously improving should remain at their current salary. Although they are not meeting the standard, they are demonstrating the right behaviors in participating in the unifying rituals, and we should work with them to reach the next level of performance.

For those employees who are below the standard and not continuously improving, we need to understand the *why* further. If their manager is actively providing them with feedback and has exhausted their coaching, then the employee is the wrong fit for our culture. This conclusion is especially correct if that employee's peers reporting to the same manager are continuously improving, meeting, or exceeding the standard. However, if the manager is not adequately providing feedback and coaching per the Standard Work, then we must repeat our line of questioning as seen in the picture below.

If their manager (in this case, the value stream manager) is actively providing the process manager with feedback and has exhausted their coaching, then the process manager is the wrong fit for our culture and must be let go. However, if the value stream manager is not adequately providing feedback and coaching per the Standard Work, then we must, once again, repeat our line of questioning. This logic goes on all the way until we reach the person at the top. If the CEO reports to a board of directors, they need to hold the CEO accountable.

If the CEO does not report to anyone, ultimately, he reports to the customers. If he does not step down, eventually, customers will vote with their dollars, and the company will suffer. For the CEO who does voluntarily step down (what the Japanese call *hara-kiri*) there is honor in doing the right thing. CEOs rarely execute this act of bravery. Who honestly would resign when they are making millions of dollars at the expense of others who they can throw under the bus? It's a sad reality, but a true one.

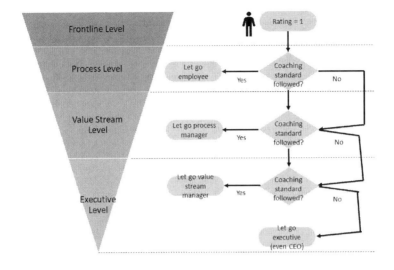

**Figure 4.14** - In a Sacred Workday culture, leaders are accountable for the Coaching and Development of their employees.

## *Bonus*

If a company meets or exceeds its' financial targets for the year, the company should share a percentage of the profit with the employees. That percentage should go into a pool and distribute according to performance ratings.

Although a Sacred Workday culture has other benefits beyond financial ones, the creation of wealth is a major one, and it motives our employees. As such, our compensation structure should be made transparent to all employees. I would go as far as to say that each employee's compensation should be made public. In a Sacred Workday culture where we tie compensation to a formula which considers the right results and the right rituals, we remove bias. By making each employee's pay visible to all, we ensure bias does not creep in, which typically has adverse effects on woman and minorities.[32] It is essential for our employees to realize that their commitment to creating a Sacred Workday culture will lead to both company and personal gain. Too many companies embark on a journey to achieve a Sacred Workday without any interest in sharing profits with their employees. It is no surprise when their efforts only yield profane results. Now that we understand the different elements of the Management System let's see what they look like at each tier.

## MANAGEMENT SYSTEM AT EACH TIER

### STANDARD WORK

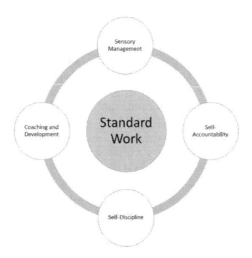

First, let's recall our definition of Standard Work: *the current best-known way to perform a process to yield the desired outcome*. It typically consists of five components:

- Required inputs to work on
- Steps and sequence of steps to transform the inputs
- Process characteristics, e.g., number of shifts, shift time, number of people, or anything else pertinent to how employees should do the work

- Process metrics, e.g., planned cycle time and acceptable amounts of inventory or Standard Work-in-progress (SWIP)
- Outcome metrics, e.g., # of units, quality

As we apply this at the various levels of our organization, the definition does not change, but instead, the lens in which we use the definition.

## Enterprise Level

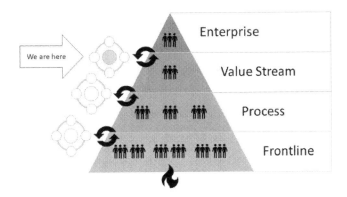

At the enterprise level, we want to look at our Standard Work less frequently, i.e., monthly, and with a lens of the entire business to understand how we are performing as an organization. Adjustments at this level are typically strategic. Let's analyze the Standard Work elements starting from the outcome metrics and working our way backward.

## Outcome Metrics

It is essential to understand the health of our business concerning ideal results and ideal rituals.

For ideal results, as we reviewed in chapter 2, we need to know our performance to:

- Revenue
- Gross margin

These key performance indicators will give the executive team some insight into the health of the business. To get a complete picture, we will also need to look at how the company is performing to ideal rituals. But how do you measure that?

An ideal rituals assessment should be developed in the form of a survey as seen below that should be administered monthly.

| # | Question | Rating | | | | | | | | | |
|---|----------|--------|---|---|---|---|---|---|---|---|---|
| 1 | We focus on creating value for the customer | 1 | 2 | 3 | 4 | 5 | 6 | 7 | 8 | 9 | 10 |
| 2 | Our team understands our company purpose and our works aligns to it | 1 | 2 | 3 | 4 | 5 | 6 | 7 | 8 | 9 | 10 |
| 3 | Teams are managed in a way that focuses on doing what is best for the value stream | 1 | 2 | 3 | 4 | 5 | 6 | 7 | 8 | 9 | 10 |
| 4 | We produce *widgets* just-in-time without over-producing | 1 | 2 | 3 | 4 | 5 | 6 | 7 | 8 | 9 | 10 |
| 5 | Defects are stopped at the source and are not pushed forward | 1 | 2 | 3 | 4 | 5 | 6 | 7 | 8 | 9 | 10 |
| 6 | When problems occur our default it to focus on the process and not blame people | 1 | 2 | 3 | 4 | 5 | 6 | 7 | 8 | 9 | 10 |
| 7 | Our team uses a scientific approach to problem solving | 1 | 2 | 3 | 4 | 5 | 6 | 7 | 8 | 9 | 10 |
| 8 | When a Challenge or Target Condition is met, we set a new one and seek perfection | 1 | 2 | 3 | 4 | 5 | 6 | 7 | 8 | 9 | 10 |
| 9 | Our management allows us to be self-accountable and to problem solve on our own | 1 | 2 | 3 | 4 | 5 | 6 | 7 | 8 | 9 | 10 |
| 10 | Our management provides us with challenges and coaches us towards achieving them | 1 | 2 | 3 | 4 | 5 | 6 | 7 | 8 | 9 | 10 |

**Figure 4.15** - A sample survey to better understand our current state of ideal rituals.

There is a lot of concern with survey fatigue. However, I often find that engaged employees don't mind providing monthly feedback, especially when they see leaders using the input to *embrace problems and transform them into continuous improvement, thus, renewing employee freshness and strength.* If there is fatigue as indicated by a low response rate, then management knows where they stand. The answer is not to stop measuring, but, instead, to deal with the root cause of why the rituals are not happening.

## Process Metrics

At the enterprise level, the process metrics are the outcome metrics of the value stream that impact revenue and gross margin, which we will explore shortly. We also want to see how the value stream is affecting ideal rituals for the organization. Thus, it's important to segment the ideal rituals assessment by value stream and by process team. By having this information, we establish a cause and effect relationship between the value stream and the business. A business is comprised of parts and is only as successful as the sum of those parts.

## Process Characteristics

At the enterprise level, it's important to understand what your value streams are, how many shifts each value stream operates, the shift times, the number of people, and any other essential attributes.

## Steps and Sequence of Steps to Transform the Inputs

The enterprise-level future state Value Stream Map serves as the standard steps and sequence of steps required to transform inputs. It is crucial to visualize both the enterprise-level current state Value Stream Map and the enterprise-level future state Value Stream Map. At the beginning of our Sacred Workday journey, this will include the support value streams and, most likely, one focus value stream. With time, we will add additional focus value streams as they become part of the strategic scope.

## Required Inputs to Work On

This last component of Standard Work may not seem relevant at the enterprise level, but that would be a mistake. Value streams in an enterprise often suffer from inferior quality parts (be they physical or digital) received from a supplier. It is crucial leadership understand what these inputs are and understand how suppliers are doing in providing the value streams what they need. I find that leadership often overlooks poor quality when the supplier has power, e.g., a broker who sells financial products for a financial services firm. It is especially important in these cases that leadership help the workers in the value stream, ensuring they get the right parts to execute their Standard Work.

## Value Stream Level

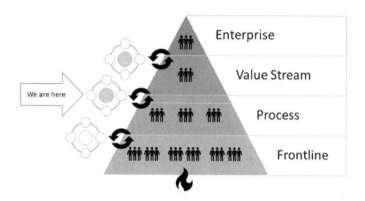

At the value stream, we want to look at our Standard Work daily to understand how we are performing as a value stream (the horizontal delivery of value to the customer).

### Outcome Metrics

At the value stream level, we need to ensure we are meeting our ideal results, which tie back to those for the enterprise. It is crucial leadership balance the metrics they use, typically around the categories of speed, quality, cost and employee morale. In other words, we want to design a value stream that is fast, gives the customer what they want, at the lowest cost possible (to reduce costs for our customers in terms of what they pay), in a way that engages our employees to *perform unifying rituals that embrace problems and transform them into continuous, thus, storing employee freshness and strength.*

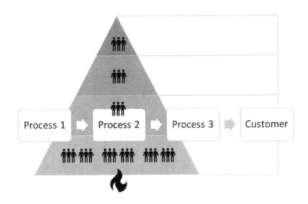

**Figure 4.16** - Value stream "horizontal" view of the organization.

| Category | Enterprise | Value Stream | Process | Frontline |
|---|---|---|---|---|
| Speed | • Revenue<br>• Gross Margin | • Lead Time (% within target)<br>• # of units produced | Work-in-Progress (WIP) | • Cycle Time<br>• WIP |
| Quality | | Defects (% of tot) | Errors (% of tot) | Errors (% of tot) |
| Cost | | • Gross Margin<br>• Overtime | Overtime | Adherence to work hours |
| Employee Morale | • Executive adherence to Leader Standard Work<br>• % of employees meeting or exceeding Standard Work<br>• # of promotions<br>• Ideal rituals survey results | • Value Stream Manager adherence to Leader Standard Work<br>• Ideal rituals survey results | Manager adherence to Leader Standard Work | Adherence to Standard Work |

**Figure 4.17** - Example of balanced metrics at each level of the organization. Note: these metrics connect from one level to another, creating alignment.

*Process Metrics*

As the chart on the previous page depicts, at the value stream level, the process metrics are the outcome metrics of the processes within the value stream. When the outcome metrics for the value stream are not performing to target, the process metrics should be observed to see where to go and see and investigate further.

*Steps and Sequence of Steps to Transform the Inputs*

The value stream-level future state Value Stream Map (whichever one of the several we are currently working towards) serves as the standard steps and sequence of steps required to transform inputs. Like the enterprise level, it is essential to visualize both the current state value stream and the desired future state Value Stream Map.

*Required Inputs to Work On*

The inputs into the value stream should also be defined to complete our Standard Work definition at the value stream level.

## Process Level

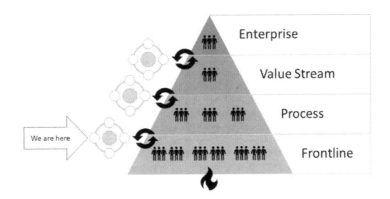

We won't break down Standard Work at the process level here since we already discussed how it is created by the frontlines using TWI methods in chapter 3. However, it is vital to summarize a few key points quickly.

Using Value Stream Mapping, we define Standard Work at the enterprise and value stream levels. We can now do so at the process level using Job Instruction Breakdown. In doing so, we enable the value stream and enterprise levels to meet their Standard Work. Once, and only once, a team defines Standard Work at the process level can we entirely build out our Management System. The Management System's primary purpose is to support adherence to Standard Work at the process level, which, in turn, will allow the value stream and, thus, the enterprise to achieve success.

The plans for the Production and Management Systems are created at the top by the executives and are cascaded down using the Catch-Ball process, as we will further explore in the next chapter. The build of both begins with the creation of Standard Work at the process level.

SENSORY MANAGEMENT

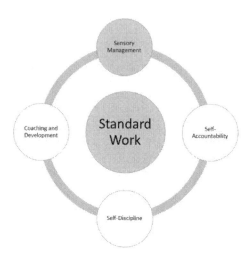

Let's recall our definition of Sensory Management: *sensory tools that allow the community to detect problems.* It is important to remember that a problem is a deviation from the Standard Work. Thus, Sensory Management at each level of the organization should display three things:

- Standard Work (which also includes Leader Standard Work and any other relevant standards such as 5S)
- Performance to Standard Work
- Self-Accountability or the person self-accountable to place a countermeasure in place

Let's review what this looks like at each level of an organization.

## Enterprise Level

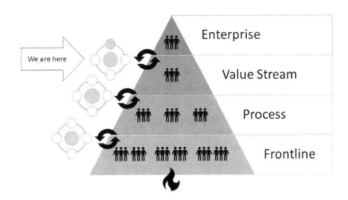

## Planning and Reflection Huddles

### Demand and Capacity Board

The first form of Sensory Management at the enterprise level is the visualization of demand and capacity. Visualizing this is critical. If a business cannot keep up with their demand, the competition will, and there will have adverse effects on the company that will make a Sacred Workday impossible to achieve.

A bar chart of forecasted demand should be displayed going out for a rolling six months with an additional six months of history (1-year total). When we reach a new month, we add a complimentary bar that represents the actual capacity. We should perform this update for each product and service. This charting will give us a sense of whether there is a gap in capacity. If there is, the manager needs to develop a capacity plan that deploys the following strategies:

- Overtime
- Reducing process cycle time via continuous improvement
- Hire and train (permanent or temp workers)
- Upskill and redeploy employees from one value-stream to

another if their demand patterns are inverted

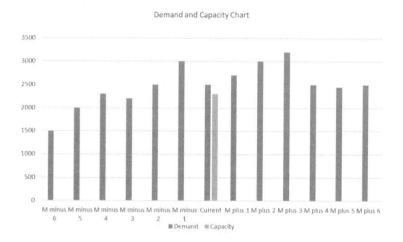

Figure 4.18 - In the above demand and capacity chart, we can see that our current capacity will not meet up-and-coming demand levels and, thus, we need to put in place some countermeasures as part of our capacity plan.

A *Job Instruction Training Timetable* (sometimes referred to as a *Skills Matrix*) should be displayed for the entire organization demonstrating which employees can work in which value streams and showing target dates for training and upskilling. At this level, employees can be moved from one value stream to another to help appropriately match capacity to demand.

Remember, the forecast for demand should correlate to targets for the Marketing and Sales team. Thus, they need to be aware of the capacity plan that the Operations team develops to create alignment, i.e., depending on whether operations has enough capacity, the Marketing and Sales team either slow down, stay the course, or speed up.

## *Performance Board*

Also, we want to look at our performance to Standard Work monthly to understand how the enterprise is progressing towards the Vision: both ideal results and ideal rituals. However, to support our daily management, there are several elements of the executive-level Performance Board that will be updated daily.

For enterprise performance, run charts are an effective way to show performance to target month-over-month for both revenue and margin. These reports can be printed or updated manually (as simple as plotting a new data point and connecting it to the previous data point with a straight line).

For the assessment of rituals, a spider chart is one effective visual to demonstrate performance to target.

We also want to display how the executives are doing concerning their Leader Standard Work. It is vital for a copy of their Leader Standard Work to be posted so everyone can see it and for us also to measure how they are performing to it. Remember, role-modeling needs to start from the top. Unlike the other metrics, this metric should be updated daily because it is one that executives can control daily. A run chart that displays the percentage of days target met can also be updated monthly to show trends.

In addition to these ideal results, it is essential to display the following information as shown in the image on the next page:

- Enterprise-level Value Stream Maps
- Value Stream daily performance
- Value Stream trend performance

I find that it is helpful to display three value streams: the initial Value Stream Map, the current state Value Stream Map, and the future state Value Stream Map that we are aspiring to. That way we know where we started from, where we are, and where we are going. I often find that the current Value Stream Map is not up-to-date.

Lastly, we should have a portion of the board that displays how the value streams in our business are performing to their outcome metrics daily. This visualization will allow us to see how our value streams are impacting our enterprise performance. As such, management will know where to go and see as part of their Leader Standard Work. For each balanced scorecard metric, we should capture the actual to target with abnormalities written in red. Also, run charts should be used to provide us with a sense of whether there are emerging themes.

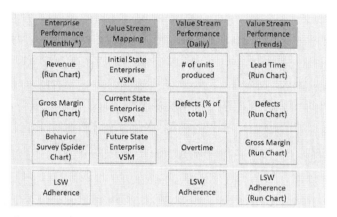

*except for LSW Adherence, which should also be updated daily

**Figure 4.19** - Sample layout of enterprise Performance Board.

Remember, the purpose of this book is not to provide specific examples of tools. It is vital that the community provide input into what means they want to use to achieve the desired rituals. In my experience, this usually translates into something simple and easy to maintain.

## _Self-Accountability Board_

Several Sensory Management tools will support Self-Accountability at the enterprise level. As we have covered, Huddles and Planned (slow thinking) are both vehicles for problems to escalate to the executive level. Although we should only expect 20% of problems to escalate to management (and even fewer to the executive level), when they do, we need a way for the executive team to take ownership. The visual tool we can use to do so is called an *Self-Accountability Board*.

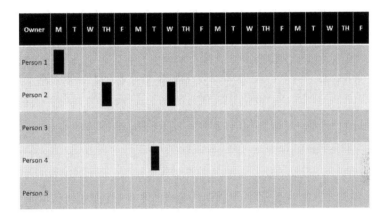

**Figure 4.20** - Sample Self-Accountability Board.

An Self-Accountability Board is a simple visual where we list all the days of the month on the x-axis and a list of potential owners, in this case, our executives and value stream managers, on the y-axis. When someone is self-accountable for a task, they write down a short description on a sticky-note and place it on the date by when they plan to complete the task. When that date arrives, if the work is complete, we remove it. If the task is not complete, we leave it where it is until the accountable employee completes it. This visualization is not intended to shame anyone, but instead, allows executives to be self-accountable.

## *Value Stream Level*

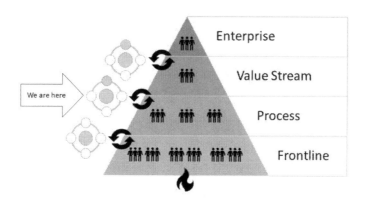

## *Planning and Reflection Huddles*

### Demand and Capacity Board

It is also essential to also understand demand and capacity at the value stream level. At this level, we will leverage the same Sensory Management tools as used at the enterprise level, just adjusted to focus on the value stream level. For example, the Job Instruction training timetable should show which employees can perform which processes. Whereas employees are moved from one value stream to another at the enterprise level, employees are transferred from one process to another at the value stream level.

### Performance Board

At the value stream level, we want to look at how we are performing in comparison to our Standard Work daily to understand how the value stream is progressing towards the Challenge.

As we go from the enterprise level to the frontline level, the frequency in which we review performance increases, and the focus of what we are trying to achieve becomes more short-term.

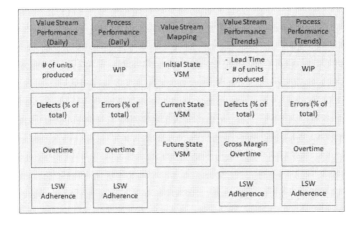

| Value Stream Performance (Daily) | Process Performance (Daily) | Value Stream Mapping | Value Stream Performance (Trends) | Process Performance (Trends) |
|---|---|---|---|---|
| # of units produced | WIP | Initial State VSM | - Lead Time<br>- # of units produced | WIP |
| Defects (% of total) | Errors (% of total) | Current State VSM | Defects (% of total) | Errors (% of total) |
| Overtime | Overtime | Future State VSM | Gross Margin Overtime | Overtime |
| LSW Adherence | LSW Adherence | | LSW Adherence | LSW Adherence |

**Figure 4.21** - Sample layout of value stream-level Performance Board.

On the value stream-level Performance Board seen above, we follow a similar format as we did at the enterprise level. Each day, we capture how the value stream does by writing our actual performance to target for our balanced scorecard metrics, i.e., production, quality, cost, and employee morale.

We do the same at the process level, allowing us to see how our processes are impacting our value stream. As a result, management will know where to go and see as part of their Leader Standard Work.

We also want to display the initial value stream-level Value Stream Map, current state Value Stream Map and future state Value Stream Map to inform us of where we were, where we are, and where we are going.

Lastly, we want to display both weekly and monthly trends for the value stream and for the processes in the form of run charts. These charts will allow us to see whether any problems experienced daily are symptomatic of a more significant problem, or just an isolated occurrence for the day based on abnormal conditions, i.e., a worker on a team got sick and didn't show up.

## Self-Accountability Board

The same category of Sensory Management for Self-Accountability that exists at the enterprise level should exist at the value stream level. However, at the value stream level, the owners should consist of the value stream manager and the various process managers. We expect to populate this board with 20% of problems escalated from each process.

## Intermediate Huddles

### Unplanned (fast thinking)

As we covered earlier in this chapter, the use of the Andon is our Standard Work for when problems arise in production. Although there is no Sensory Management at the value stream level for Unplanned (fast thinking) per se, the value stream manager is the second line of defense when the Andon is triggered, and, as a result, will need to be close to the genba to see and hear the Andon signal.

### Planned (fast thinking)

Like Unplanned (fast thinking), there is no Sensory Management at the value stream level for Planned (fast thinking) per se. However, the value stream manager will also need to be close to the Sensory Management elements at the process level, which may include a Kanban Board, Hour-by-Hour Board,  or a Kamishibai Board.

### Planned (slow thinking)

At the value stream level, we will require a *PDCA Board* which will house PDCA templates as seen on the next page.

| PDCA Template | | | | Problem: | |
|---|---|---|---|---|---|
| | | | | Why?: | |
| Date Opened: | | | | Why?: | |
| Owner: | | | | Why?: | |
| Date Escalated: | | | | Why?: | |
| New Owner: | | | | Why?: | |

| Today's Date | Plan | By when? | What do you expect? | What happened? (Check) | What did you learn? (Adjust) | Problem Solved? |
|---|---|---|---|---|---|---|
| | | | | | | |
| | | | | | | |
| | | | | | | |

Figure 4.22 - Sample PDCA Template.

This board will be the centerpiece for the coach (an executive) and the learner (the value stream manager) to go through the Coaching Kata ritual.

At this level, the Target Condition is the future state we are currently working towards, i.e., stabilization, flow, pull or leveling the load and mix. We depict the Actual Condition as a current state Value Stream Map that should be kept up-to-date and trend charts. We display all this information on the value stream-level Performance Board.

At this level, problems will be defined on the PDCA template and escalated by process managers to the value stream manager (it physically moves from the process-level PDCA Board to the value stream-level PDCA Board). Before this escalation, however, the process manager must first:

a) Understand the problem
b) Understand the root-cause of the problem
c) Exhaust experimentation at the process level to try and solve the problem.

Recall, escalations should only account for 20% of the total issues the frontline employees experience at the process level. As such, it is essential the value stream manager only accept an escalation if we meet the three criteria previously mentioned. In doing so, the value stream manager demonstrates the Shingo principle of *respect for the individual* by asking process managers to think and become problem solvers. The executive should use the same logic and only take ownership of a PDCA template if the value stream manager has also met the three criteria highlighted above (although in this case, the template will stay on the value stream-level PDCA Board). At any given time, I recommend that a value stream manager only works on one problem per process in their value stream. Most of the time, multiple operations are experiencing issues due to the same root cause.

## Process Level

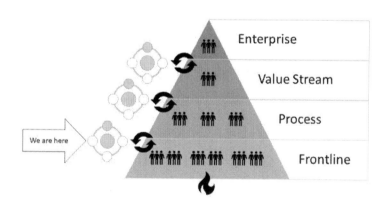

The closer we get to the frontline, the more frequent our Sensory Management must be updated to allow for our frontline employees to act like the reflex arc. At the process level, we want to update Sensory Management in real-time and intra-daily with a focus on achieving a more near-term Target Condition.

## Standard Work

Our focal point of Sensory Management at the process level is Standard Work. At the process level, we are at the genba. Thus, our Sensory Management must be centered around achieving the ultimate task-at-hand: delivering value to our customers. Standard Work is what provides management with visibility into our ability to do so, revealing abnormalities. Thus, it should be visible always. It is important to note that the entire Management System, at each level, from the frontline to the enterprise, will be constructed to support the Standard Work at the process level.

## Planning and Reflection Huddles

### Demand and Capacity Board

At the value stream and enterprise level, demand and capacity is mostly a strategic activity, whereas, at the process level, it is more practical. On any given day, demand and capacity will both fluctuate. Thus, it is vital that our Sensory Management allow our process managers to plan, check and adjust appropriately through the use of several forms of Sensory Management, individually:

- On the demand-side
  - Kanban Board
  - Hour-by-Hour Board
  - Kamishibai board

- On the capacity-side
  - Attendance
  - Assignments
  - Job Instruction Training Timetable, a.k.a. Skills Matrix

As we discussed earlier, the Kanban Board, Hour-by-Hour Board, and Kamishibai Board all help the process manager visualize which tasks and the number of tasks the team must complete for the day.

The attendance, assignments and Skills Matrix provide the process manager with visibility into how much capacity the team has (or doesn't) to complete those tasks. The attendance shows who plans to work for the day and who showed up. The assignments show who is working on what. The Skills Matrix confirms those who are assigned to work on specific tasks have the required skills to do so. Whenever there is not enough capacity to meet the demand, the process manager needs to adjust appropriately, i.e., request appropriately skilled employees from other processes that have additional capacity for the day, step in and work to help the team out, and/or have frontline employees work overtime.

| Attendance | | | | | | | | | | | |
|---|---|---|---|---|---|---|---|---|---|---|---|
| Employee | In / Out | M | | T | | W | | TH | | F | |
| | | P | A | P | A | P | A | P | A | P | A |
| Employee 1 | ● | ● | ● | ● | | ● | | ● | | ● | |
| Employee 2 | ● | ◔ | ● | ◔ | | ◔ | | ◔ | | ◔ | |
| Employee 3 | ◔ | ◔ | ◔ | ◔ | | ◔ | | ◔ | | ◔ | |
| Employee 4 | ◔ | ◔ | ◔ | ◔ | | ◔ | | ◔ | | ◔ | |
| Employee 5 | ◔ | ◔ | ◔ | ◔ | | ◔ | | ◔ | | ◔ | |
| Supervisor | ◔ | ◔ | ◔ | ◔ | | ◔ | | ◔ | | ◔ | |

● Out-of-office

◔ In office

**Figure 4.23** - Sample Attendance.

| Assignments | | | | | | |
|---|---|---|---|---|---|---|
| Hour | Employee | | | | | |
| | Employee 1 | Employee 2 | Employee 3 | Employee 4 | Employee 5 | Supervisor |
| 8-9 | Process 1 | Process 2 | Process 1 | Process 1 | Process 3 | |
| 9-10 | Process 1 | Process 2 | Process 1 | Process 1 | Process 3 | |
| 10-11 | Process 1 | Process 2 | Process 1 | Process 1 | Process 3 | |
| 11-12 | Process 1 | Process 2 | Process 1 | Process 1 | Process 3 | |
| 12-1 | Process 1 | Process 3 | Process 1 | Process 1 | Process 2 | |
| 1-2 | Process 1 | Process 3 | Process 1 | Process 1 | Process 2 | |
| 2-3 | Process 1 | Process 3 | Process 1 | Process 1 | Process 2 | |
| 3-4 | Process 1 | Process 3 | Process 1 | Process 1 | Process 2 | |
| 4-5 | Process 1 | Process 3 | Process 1 | Process 1 | Process 2 | |

**Figure 4.24** - Sample Assignments.

Although the above strategies make sense in the short-term, it is vital that a process manager lead *unifying rituals that embrace problems and transform them into continuous improvement, thus, restoring employee freshness and strength.* In doing so, we create additional capacity through the efficiencies gained to achieve our purpose.

| Skill Matrix | | | | | | |
|---|---|---|---|---|---|---|
| Process | Employee | | | | | |
| | Employee 1 | Employee 2 | Employee 3 | Employee 4 | Employee 5 | Supervisor |
| Process 1 | ● | ● | ● | ● | ● | ● |
| Process 2 | 3/9 ● | ● | 3/9 ● | ● | ● | ● |
| Process 3 | 4/9 ● | ● | 4/9 ● | ● | ● | ● |

● Not Skilled

● Skilled

**Figure 4.25** - Sample Skills Matrix.

## *Performance Board*

At the process level, we also have a Performance Board to show us how we did for the day as seen on the next page.

The Performance Board should be updated at the end of the day and is the focal point for the Reflection Huddle. Specifically, the Performance Board shows us whether we were able to achieve our Target Condition based on the morning's plan. The primary metric the process team will focus on is work in progress (WIP), which is an indicator of whether the team is working at a pace that keeps up with customer demand. The Performance Board will also keep track of quality (errors committed by the group that impacted the downstream process), and overtime to ensure the team meet's the WIP target healthily.

The Performance Board will also display trend charts to give the team a sense of their performance over a period.

Most teams cover multiple processes. *In Learning to See*, Rother and Shook refer to this as a *loop*. Thus, in those cases, it is also important to post several loop-specific "value stream" maps that show where the loop started from, where it's at, and where it is going. This visualization continues to build the alignment.

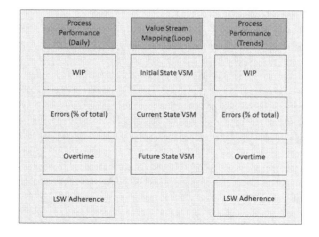

**Figure 4.26** - Sample Performance Board at the process level.

## Self-Accountability Board

The same category of Sensory Management for Self-Accountability that exists at the enterprise and value stream levels should exist at the process level. However, at the process level, the owners should consist of the process manager and the various team members. This visual board will be the place to capture any task, which we expect to include 80% of problems (our reflex arc!). At this level, we should also replace days on the x-axis with hours or the appropriately pitch as Self-Accountability will happen more often and with quick turn-around.

## Intermediate Huddles

### Unplanned (fast thinking)

The Andon is our primary tool that allows for Unplanned (fast thinking). We have already covered this, but it's important to reiterate that the use of the Andon depends entirely on how management reacts to when it is triggered. As we stated previously, we should capture the number of times the Andon is triggered. If this number is too low, management should go to genba to see whether employees are following Standard Work. In the case that they are not, there may be a need for retraining or management to self-reflect on their use of Humble Inquiry.

## Planned (fast thinking)

We also already covered the three primary tools for Planned (fast thinking): Kanban Board, Hour-by-Hour Board, and the Kamishibai Board. Like the Andon, it is essential that process managers ensure these forms of Sensory Management are up-to-date. Managers will only be able to do so if they are self-disciplined and follow their Leader Standard Work. If they do not, these tools will quickly become obsolete.

## Planned (slow thinking)

At the process level, like at the value stream level, we will also require a PDCA Board which will house PDCA templates. This board will be the centerpiece for the coach (this time the value stream manager) and the learner (this time the process manager) to go through the Coaching Kata ritual.

At this level, the Target Condition should connect to the future state we are currently working towards, i.e., stabilization, flow, pull or leveling the load and mix. The Actual Condition is captured on the Performance Board and through direct observation of the process by the process manager at the genba.

At this level, teams will identify problems on the Performance Board as gaps or actuals below target. Through the use of our Management System, we should be able to quickly adjust and close the gap on certain problems quickly. However, when we cannot and there is a reoccurring problem, a manager should create a new PDCA template as seen in the image on page 135.

The 5-why analysis should be used to drill-down to the root cause of why this gap exists. The Pareto analysis and direct observation at the genba will help guide this. Once, and only once, the root-cause is understood, we can move onto experimentation. The process manager, as the learner, will work with frontline employees to conduct experiments. Through experimentation, the process manager and team should solve for 80% of the problems. They should escalate the remaining 20% when, and only when, they exhaust experimentation. Again, we want the value stream manager to coach our process managers to think for themselves and become problem solvers to achieve a Sacred Workday.

## Frontline Level

At the frontline level, it is essential to have simple Sensory Management, which typically consists of the following:

- Job-Aids
- Personal Kanban Board
- Andon
- Suggestions

At the frontline, employees should spend 95% of their time in production. As a result of being trained using Job Instruction, they should be well-trained on how to do their work before entering production. There are always elements of the job that will be very difficult to do, especially in intricate knowledge work. As such, Job-Aids should be readily available to assist workers, e.g., decision trees, if-then diagrams, etc.

In environments where employees cannot visualize their inventory, a personal Kanban Board is vital to help them manage their inventory. More importantly, through use of a personal Kanban Board, employees make inventory visual to their managers. This visualization reveals their capacity so that managers can adjust and redistribute work when necessary to avoid muri.

Lastly, it is essential the frontline employees have a voice to make suggestions for experimentation. Although they spend most of their time in production, they need to be active in identifying problems, root-cause analysis, and contributing ideas for experiments. This sort of focused engagement is very different than typical employee suggestions programs that, too often, lack structure. Such programs quickly lose steam as employees submit a batch of ideas, only to see them go nowhere or, even worse, get implemented without knowledge of the problem. In a Sacred Workday culture, employees are aware of the problem, the gap, and offer/implement suggestions that are meaningful.

## Auditory, Visual and Tactile Reminders

In my experience, it is easy to lose the Self-Discipline of meeting to Huddle. The profane habits previously developed are difficult to break and a Sacred Workday does not come easy. As such, the use of auditory, visual, and tactile reminders is a must. At the Huddle start time, an alarm should make a sound, a light should flash, or wearable technology should buzz, signaling to employees that it is time to meet. As I stated before, the alarm should be reoccurring until someone shuts it off and that should only happen once a critical mass has gathered to Huddle.

An alarm, light or vibration should also signal the end time of the Huddle. Then, everyone should return to production to ensure we can keep up with our customer demand. The alarm reinforces the brevity of the Huddle and the need to follow an agenda.

With the first three elements of our Management System in place, we now switch focus to the element that will ensure these first three happen ritually to make a Sacred Workday a reality.

SELF-ACCOUNTABILITY

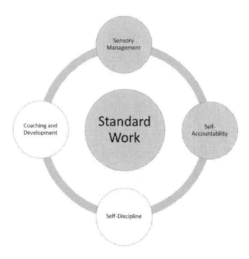

Self-Accountability should start from those closest to the work if our business is to mimic the reflex arc. With Standard Work and Sensory Management in place at each level of the organization, we now have the foundational tools in place to allow for this. Now we need protected and structured time where we *perform unifying rituals that embrace problems and transform them into continuous improvement, thus, restoring employee freshness and strength.* Let's explore what that looks like starting at the process level this time.

## Process Level

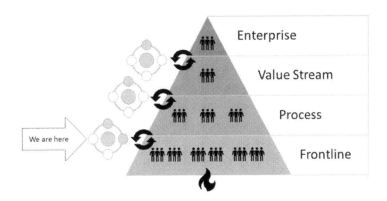

## Planning Huddle

At the process level, Self-Accountability begins with the Planning Huddle, which should happen before the start of each shift.  Let's recall the simple agenda:

- What are our purpose, Vision, and Challenge?
- What is the Target Condition? (for the day)
- What is our plan to be successful?
  - Attendance
  - **Assignments**
  - Key communications

From a perspective of Self-Accountability, the most critical part of the Planning Huddle is the assigning of work as bolded in the agenda above.

This allocation of responsibility may seem contradictory to the notion of Self-Accountability, but it is not. Team members must first know what is expected of them if they are to be self-accountable. By assigning work, a manager exhibits the Shingo principle of *respect for the individual.* For a manager to do this effectively, first,  they must understand what jobs there are, followed by how they are supposed to do them, i.e., the Standard Work.

## Intermediate Huddles

### Planned and Unplanned (fast thinking)

After the Planning Huddle, the next planned opportunity for Self-Accountability happens at each of the scheduled pitches, i.e., Planned (fast thinking), at which point, frontline employees should update the Hour-by-Hour Board, Kamishibai Board, or Kanban Board. Each pitch is an opportunity for employees to be self-accountable to problems that they encounter.

For example, let's say the team is performing to takt; however, one task on the Kamishibai Board did not get completed. When the team gathers at the pitch, they notice the employee who owned that task is behind on their work as seen on their personal Kanban Board. At this point, an employee who is ahead of their work could be self-accountable and take ownership of the task on the Kamishibai Board to help their peer. The employee that assists would record this countermeasure on the Self-Accountability Board and, in this scenario, the process manager would not have to get involved in delegating.

If an employee cannot follow the Standard Work at any point in time, they should always be self-accountable to trigger the Andon. This behavior is their ultimate responsibility.

*So, what is the role of the process manager?*

The process manager's role is to ensure, at each pitch, employees are updating Sensory Management and being self-accountable. They also ensure that the Andon is triggered when Standard Work is not followed. In other words, the process manager ensures the Self-Discipline. They do so via Leader Standard Work.

### Planned (slow thinking)

In addition to Planned and Unplanned (fast thinking), occasionally, frontline employees will be brought into Planned (slow thinking) to leverage their knowledge of the process.

## Reflection Huddle

The last planned opportunity for Self-Accountability is the Reflection Huddle at the end of each shift. Let's recall the agenda:

- What is the Target Condition? (for the shift)
- What is our Actual Condition?
    - **What countermeasures did we put in place?**
    - **What did we expect to happen?**
    - **What happened?**
    - **What did we learn?**
- What problems got in our way?
- **What additional countermeasures will we put in place?**
    - **Who will be self-accountable?**
    - **What do we expect to happen?**
- **By when will they be put in place?**
- Is there anyone we should recognize?

As highlighted above, the questions that are in bold are focused on Self-Accountability, with the first group focusing on checking to see if employees were self-accountable and the second grouping creating self-accountability moving forward. If employees were not self-accountable, there is an opportunity to understand *why* while always assuming there is a valid reason. If an employee simply forgot or did not hold up their end of the bargain, the Huddle serves as a robust social reminder (nothing feels worse than letting down your team).

With protected and structured time in place, we now have the needed infrastructure for the reflex arc. However, this doesn't mean we will be able to contain all problems to the frontline and process level. We should expect 20% to require help from the value stream level.

## Value Stream and Enterprise Levels

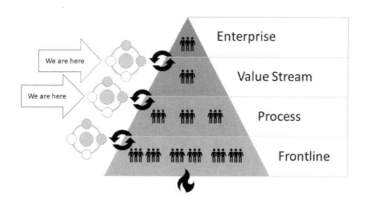

At the value stream and enterprise level, there is too much redundancy with the process level to go through Self-Accountability in full detail. However, we'll briefly cover the following two critical ways problems get escalated:

- Via Planning and Reflection Huddles
- Via Planned (slow thinking)

Upon completing the Planning Huddle at the process level, the process managers should attend the Planning Huddle at the value stream level. This subsequent Huddle is the opportunity to escalate problems they could not solve. These kinds of problems typically involve the need for horizontal collaboration, i.e., quality issues from an upstream process or the need for more capacity from another team with properly crossed-trained employees. Upon completing this Planning Huddle, the value stream manager should attend the enterprise Planning Huddle where other value stream managers will also be in attendance. Value stream managers should escalate an even smaller subset of problems to this level. This same cadence should happen at the end of the shift via Reflection Huddles.

The other way for problems to escalate is via Planned (slow thinking). At the process level, if the process manager, i.e., the learner, has exhausted experiments and cannot progress, the value stream manager, i.e., the coach, can step in and take ownership of advancing experimentation. At the value stream level, the same logic applies. If the value stream manager, i.e., the learner, has exhausted experiments and cannot progress, the executive, i.e., the coach, can step in and take ownership.

The same tools, i.e., the Performance Board, PDCA Board, Self-Accountability Board, will be used to support these unifying rituals.

## SELF-DISCIPLINE

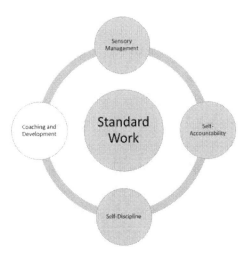

Self-Discipline starts with executive leadership. Lack of Self-Discipline at the top is the number one reason why businesses remain profane. If we recall, Self-Discipline is achieved using Leader Standard Work: *standardized, protected time that allows us to perform unifying rituals that embrace problems and transform them into continuous improvement, thus, restoring employee freshness and strength.* If we also recall, Leader Standard Work seeks to ensure:

- The person performing Leader Standard Work, at their level:
  - Develops and maintains Standard Work
  - Keeps Sensory Management up-to-date
  - Leads Planning/Reflection Huddles
  - Is Self-Accountability and responsive to escalations
  - Coaches and develops employees
- At the levels below, goes to genba to ensure:
  - Standard Work is developed and maintained
  - Sensory Management is up-to-date
  - Self-Accountability is happening
  - Coaching and Development of employees is occurring
  - Managers are practicing Self-Discipline (performing Leader Standard Work)

Let's look at what this looks like at each level of the organization.

## Enterprise Level

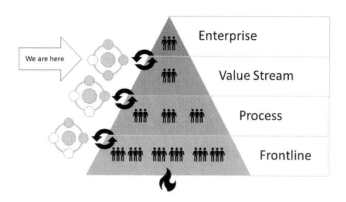

At the enterprise level, executives should dedicate **two hours** of their day to Leader Standard Work. They should spend the remaining time on strategic matters that will allow for the business to have a competitive edge in the marketplace.

They should split the two hours with one hour dedicated to the enterprise level and one hour devoted to visiting the genba at the levels below.

At their level, executives should spend most of the hour on Self-Accountability, and coaching and developing others. Developing Standard Work will happen at the beginning of the year and updating visual management should be minimum.

At the level below, executives should take time to visit value streams, processes within those value streams, and frontline employees within those processes. Sensory Management should direct them to go and see where there is a need as they will not be able to go everywhere in their business, especially if they are a larger organization. In the beginning of our journey to achieve a Sacred Workday, this can be awkward as the levels below may or may not have Sensory Management set up. However, this should not deter leadership. They should still get into the habit of going to the genba. If Sensory Management is not set up, then this should be the focus of their coaching. You can't manage what you can't see.

## *Value Stream Level*

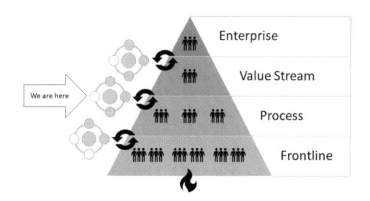

At the value stream level, the value stream manager should dedicate **four hours** to Leader Standard Work. One potential way of structuring this is seen in the table below.

|  | Dedicated Time (hours) |
|---|---|
| **At the value stream level** |  |
| Develop and maintain Standard Work | As needed |
| Update Sensory Management | .5 |
| Planning / Reflection Huddles | 1 |
| Work on Self-Accountability | .75 |
| Coach and develop employees | .75 |
| **At the process and frontline level** |  |
| Go to the genba | 1 |

Like executives, the value stream managers should also leverage Sensory Management to determine which processes to focus their genba walks on.

## Process Level

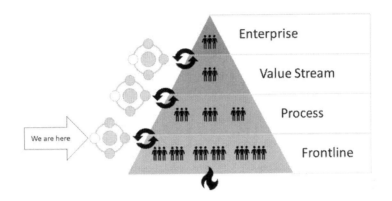

At the process level, the process manager should dedicate **six hours** to Leader Standard Work. At this level, Leader Standard Work comprises most of a process manager's workday.

Like the value stream managers, process managers should also leverage Sensory Management to determine which frontline employees to focus their genba walks on. This time can be spent, as we will explore in the next chapter, observing problems, countermeasures, or retraining where necessary.

| | Dedicated Time (hours) |
|---|---|
| **At the process level** | |
| Develop and maintain Standard Work | As needed |
| Update Sensory Management | .5 |
| Planning / Reflection Huddles | 1 |
| Work on Self-Accountability | .75 |
| Coach and develop employees | .75 |
| **At the frontline level** | |
| Go to the genba | 3 |

## COACHING AND DEVELOPMENT

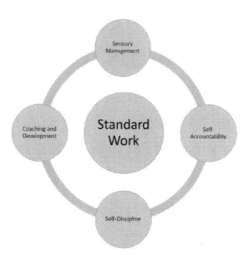

For Coaching and Development to happen at each level, we need a development plan. Let's see what that looks like at each level.

## Enterprise Level

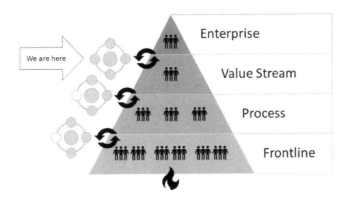

At the enterprise level, each executive, including the owner/CEO should have a development plan that consists of:

- Outcome metrics (community success)
- Process metrics (personal success that enables community success)
- Process characteristics (the way in which the executive is expected to work, i.e., Leader Standard Work)
- Ideal rituals (the way in which the executive is expected to behave)

Outcome metrics equate to the financial metrics of the entire organization. Process metrics equate to the performance of the value streams. Process characteristics equate to the executive's adherence to Leader Standard Work. And, lastly, ideal rituals equate to how executives behave relative to the Shingo principles.

For CEOs who report to a board, it is critical they have a development plan. In the case the CEO does not report to anyone, an outside coach or advisor can be leveraged to provide coaching on how the CEO is performing to the development plan. This relationship would also require that coach or advisor be knowledgeable of a Sacred Workday culture and visit the company periodically to observe the CEO. I highly recommend CEOs find an outside coach if this is the case. It is crucial everyone be a coach and have a coach in a Sacred Workday culture.

## *Value Stream Level*

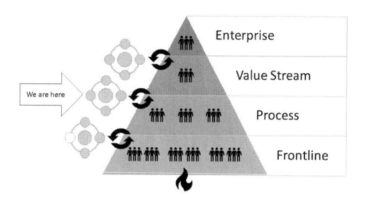

At the value stream level, outcome metrics equate to the outcome metrics for the value stream, process metrics equate to the performance of processes within the value stream, process characteristics equate to the value stream manager's adherence to Leader Standard Work and ideal rituals are the behaviors we expect the value stream manager to exhibit in accordance with the Shingo principles.

## Process Level

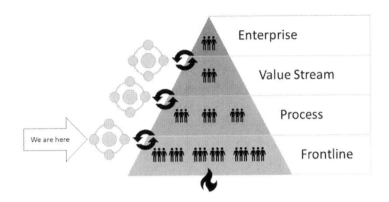

At the process level, the outcome metrics equate to the outcome metrics for the process, the process metrics equate to how we measure the process in real-time, e.g., cycle time, the process characteristics equates to the process manager's adherence to Leader Standard Work, and lastly, the ideal rituals are how the process manager behaves relevant to the Shingo principles.

## Frontline Level

At the frontline level, the outcome metrics equate to their individual outcome metrics, the process metrics relate to their individual metrics on how we measure the process in real-time, the process characteristics equates to the frontline employee's adherence to Standard Work, and lastly, the ideal rituals are how the frontline employee behaves relevant to the Shingo principles.

It is essential to recognize the connection between the development plans, from the frontline level all the way up to the enterprise level, as there is a cause-and-effect relationship. In other words, if the frontlines fail, it reflects their management.

We have reached a pivotal moment in our journey. We have discussed all the components that make up a Sacred Workday: both the Production System and the Management System. Now we will consider the unifying rituals required to build these components and, also, to put them to use to achieve a Sacred Workday.

# 4 | SUMMARY

- David Mann's *Creating a Lean Culture: Tools to Sustain Lean Conversions* serves as a standard for Lean Management System that we seek to build upon.
- Our Management System consists of 5 core elements:
    - Standard Work
    - Sensory Management
    - Self-Accountability
    - Self-Discipline
    - Coaching and Development
- Standard Work is the *current best-known way to perform a process to yield the desired outcome*. It typically consists of five components:
    - Required inputs to work on
    - Steps and sequence of steps to transform the inputs
    - Process characteristics, e.g., number of shifts, shift time, number of people, or anything else pertinent to how employees should do the work
    - Process metrics, e.g., planned cycle time and acceptable amounts of inventory or Standard Work-in-progress (SWIP)
    - Outcome metrics, e.g., # of units, quality
- Standard Work is foundational to the Management System.
- We define Sensory Management as *sensory tools that allow the community to detect problems*.
- We define Self-Accountability as *structured time where we perform unifying rituals that embrace problems and transform them into continuous improvement, thus, restoring employee freshness and strength*.
- Self-Accountability is when our frontline employees act like the reflex arc.
- There are several opportunities throughout the day that allow for Self-Accountability, including:
    - Planning Huddle

- Intermediate Huddles
  - Unplanned (fast thinking)
  - Planned (fast thinking)
  - Planned (slow thinking)
- Reflection Huddle
- Self-Discipline ensures the other elements of the Management System are working.
- The primary tool for Self-Discipline is Leader Standard Work.
- Leader Standard Work is *standardized, and protected time that allows us to perform unifying rituals that embrace problems and transform them into continuous improvement, thus, restoring employee freshness and strength.*
- Coaching and Development is the way we grow our people.
- The GROW model is a framework that helps us do so and stands for Goal, Reality, Obstacles and Way Forward.
- A development plan is the primary tool to create the goal.
- One-on-one coaching and the Feedback Model are tools that allow us to discuss progress to the development plan with direct reports. This conversation occurs regularly (at least monthly) to demonstrate the Shingo principle of *respect for the individual.*
- The Management System must exist at each level of the business, from the enterprise level, down to the frontline level. This construction allows for alignment.

# 4 | EXERCISE

- List the elements of a Management System that are currently in place in our organization at each level, i.e., enterprise, value stream, process, frontline.
- Can everyone see how you are performing to Standard Work at any given time at these different levels?
- Is there Self-Accountability in our business?
- Is there Self-Discipline in our business?
- Is there coaching and developing in our business? How often does it take place?

# 5 | RITUALS

1 | Leadership
1. Building Trust

2 | Vision
2. Ideal Results
3. Ideal Behaviors

3 | Production System
4. Enterprise Level
6. Value Stream Level
8. Process Level

4 | Management System
5. Enterprise Level
7. Value Stream Level
9. Process Level

5 | Rituals
10. Rituals

6 | Growth

## RITUALS

Up until now, we have created a blueprint for how to create a Sacred Workday. However, we have not built. That begins now. Individually, we must develop our Vision, our Production System, our Management System, and, most importantly, start to perform the unifying rituals that will allow us to realize our purpose.

Rituals are *proven routines that yield the desired outcome*; in this case, creating a Sacred Workday where we *perform unifying rituals that embrace problems and transform them into continuous improvement, thus, restoring employee freshness and strength.*

All our rituals follow the Plan Do Check Adjust or PDCA pattern but are done at different intervals and with a different focus.

## INTERVALS

The following image provides an overview of our rituals and the intervals in which they occur, which we will further explore in the remainder of this chapter.

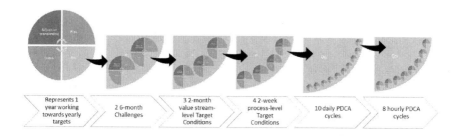

**Figure 5.1** - PDCA cycles within PDCA cycles that create alignment from the enterprise level to the frontline level.

## YEARLY PDCA

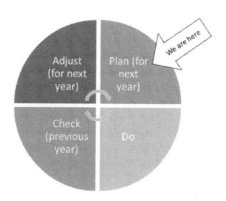

**Figure 5.2** - Yearly PDCA

Each year it is essential to reflect upon how we did (check) and make sure we apply what we learned to our strategic plan for the following year (adjust, plan). Ideally, this reflection should be kicked off *six weeks before the end of the year* so that experimentation towards next year's goals can begin on day one.

## Production System

The image below highlights a five-day working session for the executive team to plan for the year. This workshop focuses on the enterprise purpose, ideal results, ideal rituals, and the Production System (elements 2, 3, and 4 of our torii).

| Day 1 | Day 2 | Day 3 | Day 4 | Day 5 |
|---|---|---|---|---|
| ❑ Kickoff<br>❑ Review Purpose<br>❑ Review Financial Current State<br>❑ Review Financial Future State (Ideal Results)<br>❑ Review of current year's initiatives<br>❑ Select focus value stream(s) | ❑ Create Enterprise-Level Current State Value Stream Map | ❑ Create Enterprise-Level Future State Value Stream Map<br>❑ Create action plan for value stream transformation | ❑ Review Shingo Principles<br>❑ Define Ideal Rituals | ❑ Create Vision |

Figure 5.3 - Five-Day workshop to create the enterprise-level Production System.

Before the workshop, the executive team needs to do pre-work. Specifically:

- The head of finances should generate reports showing the current state of how the business is financially performing.
- The CEO (and/or board / shareholders) should determine how they want the business to perform financially for the next five years.
- Each executive should gather a summary of the current year's initiatives for which they were accountable, including whether they yielded the intended results and, more importantly, what lessons were learned.
- Someone should own conducting a product/service value stream family analysis which allows us to select with

product/service value stream to focus on, i.e., our focus value stream.

- Someone should also own creating targets for the value stream to achieve for the year (Challenge #2) with a 6-month intermediate target (Challenge #1).

With this information available, day one will focus on ensuring the executive team understands the business's purpose, has clarity on what ideal results we are trying to achieve and selects a focus value stream. Most likely, there will not be value stream managers in place, as this is new thinking concerning how we manage. Thus, the executives should also discuss who will be the value steam managers.

On days two and three, the executive team will focus on creating an enterprise-level current and future state Value Stream Map.

On day four, the executive team will define ideal rituals that will enable us to achieve our ideal results healthily.

Finally, day five will bring all the elements together as a Vision that the executive team can share with the rest of the business.

## Management System

Once the executives complete this workshop, it's essential for them to switch focus to the Management System (element 5 of our torii) via another five-day working session as seen on the next page.

We have already highlighted how to create the elements highlighted in the table. What is important to note is that the Sensory Management, in this case, a Demand and Capacity Board, a Performance Board, and an Self-Accountability Board, should all be placed in a location that is visible for all employees to see. This public display will initiate the desired role-modeling we want to see from the top.

| Day 1 | Day 2 | Day 3 | Day 4 | Day 5 |
|---|---|---|---|---|
| ❑ Create Sensory Management | ❑ Create Self-Discipline (Leader Standard Work) | ❑ Create Development Plan | ❑ Initiate Catch-ball Process<br>❑ Vision<br>❑ Production System<br>❑ Management System | ❑ Continue Catch-Ball Process<br>❑ Development Plans |

**Figure 5.4** - Five-day workshop to create the enterprise-level Management System.

## Catch-Ball

On days four and five, executives initiate the Catch-Ball process. As the name implies, the executive team cascades down the Vision for the enterprise and development plans for value stream managers. We dedicate two full days because it is vital that there is clarity on where we are going before starting to build at the value stream level. Once there is, it then becomes the responsibility of the value stream managers to react with how they plan on achieving the yearly targets for the enterprise, both from a Production System and Management System stand-point.

## 6-MONTH PDCA

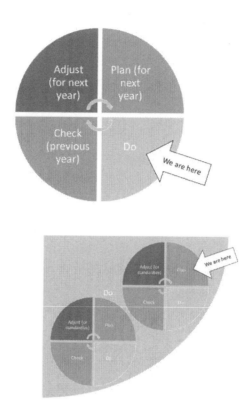

**Figure 5.5** - Two 6-month PDCA cycles at the value stream level, embedded into the larger 1-year PDCA cycle at the enterprise level.

### *Production System*

Now that we have an enterprise-level plan, we need to develop our value stream plan for both the Production System (element 6 of our torii) and Management System (element 7 of our torii). If you recall our earlier discussion in chapter 3, this will happen concurrently for four value streams initially: Market and Sell, Hire and Onboard, Train, and the focus value stream that has a significant impact on our ideal results.

Once the value stream manager understands the enterprise Vision and the value stream targets, their next step should be to formulate a team for Value Stream Mapping. The team typically consists of a process manager from each process in the value stream (usually 3-5 since process managers manage multiple processes).

> *But I thought Lean was led by the frontline employees?*
>
> A failure mode in most Lean journeys is that they select frontline employees to create the value stream-level Challenge. This does not work. Frontline employees do not have end-to-end knowledge of the value stream and rarely will design a Challenge that exists outside of their knowledge threshold. This is the job of management. The frontline employees will be involved in designing how we reach the Challenge, at which point we will heavily rely upon their knowledge of the process.

These individuals will go through the 5-day workshop as seen on the next page with the goal of creating the first value stream Challenge to be achieved in 6-months.

On day one, it is essential to review the enterprise Vision. Although we discussed this in the previous week, it is crucial to continually refer to it to ensure there is alignment in the activity we are doing; in this case, Value Stream Mapping. The facilitator should provide participants with an overview of how to current state map, after which, they will begin to map the current state.

On day two, they will continue to work on the current state value stream, visiting the genba as needed. At the end of the day, all the value streams will come together to share their current state Value Stream Map. This gathering will create horizontal alignment between the various value streams.

On day three, participants will be given an overview of the five future state Value Stream Mapping principles and will begin to create the future state Value Stream Map.

| Day 1 | Day 2 | Day 3 | Day 4 | Day 5 |
|---|---|---|---|---|
| ❏ Kickoff<br>❏ Enterprise Vision<br>❏ Overview of Value Stream Mapping<br>❏ Create Current State Value Stream Map | ❏ Continue to Create Current State Value Stream Map (make sure to visit the genba!)<br>❏ Share across value streams | ❏ Overview of Value Stream Mapping future state guiding principles<br>❏ Create Future State Value Stream Map | ❏ Continue to Create Future State Value Stream Map<br>❏ Share across value streams | ❏ Create Value Stream Production System plan<br>❏ Share across value streams |

Figure 5.6 - Five-Day workshop to create Value stream-level Production System.

On day four, they will finalize the future state Value Stream Map. The value stream managers will share these maps with their peers across the various value streams.

Finally, on day five, participants will create a Production System plan which will include a series of value stream Target Conditions the process level will strive towards. Each value stream manager will also share these plans with their peers across the various value streams.

## Management System

Upon completion of the value stream Production System plan, it is vital to switch focus to creating the Management System that will support the Production System. Most organizations who embark on a Sacred Workday journey ignore this transition, and, thus, never achieve ideal behaviors. It is not necessary for the process managers to be part of this as they have teams to manage. It does make sense, however, for the value stream managers to go through the workshop below together.

There is an overview of what that five-day workshop looks like on the following page. This agenda is the same as that at the enterprise level, however, at this level the value stream managers are playing Catch-Ball with process managers, cascading down the value stream-level Management System and development plans. Note: The Production System does not have to be cascaded as the process managers were part of constructing it.

| Day 1 | Day 2 | Day 3 | Day 4 | Day 5 |
|---|---|---|---|---|
| ❏ Create Sensory Management | ❏ Create Self-Discipline (Leader Standard Work) | ❏ Create Development Plan | ❏ Initiate Catch-ball Process<br>❏ Management System | ❏ Continue Catch-Ball Process<br>❏ Development Plans |

**Figure 5.7** - Five-day workshop to create the value stream-level Management System.

## 2-Month PDCA

If we recall, our value stream-level future state Value Stream Map identified three distinct Target Conditions:

1. Stabilize
2. Create flow
3. Pull and level the load and mix

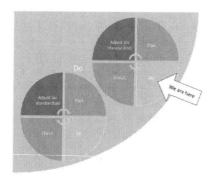

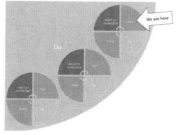

**Figure 5.8** - Three 2-month PDCA cycles at the value stream level, embedded into the more substantial 6-month PDCA cycle at the value stream level.

## *Production System*

Although I allow two months to achieve each of these, it usually doesn't work that way. Stabilization is not easy to obtain. Thus, it may make sense to have 3-month, 2-month, and 1-month Target

Conditions to stabilize, create flow, and pull and level the load and mix respectively. For simplicity, let's proceed to assume we allow 2-months for each.

Although we have defined Target Conditions at a high level for the value stream, we now need to expand upon those Target Conditions with more detail at the process level.

To do so, we will leverage a 5-day workshop highlighted below.

| Day 1 | Day 2 | Day 3 | Day 4 | Day 5 |
|-------|-------|-------|-------|-------|
| ❏ Kickoff<br>❏ Review Future State Value Stream Map<br>❏ Overview of TWI<br>❏ Understand Current State Process | ❏ Create Target Condition Draft #1 – Job Instruction Breakdown | ❏ Create Target Condition Draft #2 – 5S | ❏ Create Target Condition Draft #3 – Refine<br>❏ Create Training Timetable | ❏ Begin to train |

Figure 5.9 - Five-day workshop to determine the first process-level Target Condition.

As described in chapter 3, this is the right time for the process manager to leverage those who know the work best from our frontlines.

## Management System

Once we have created our first Target Condition, we are ready to shift gears to create our Management System via the five-day workshop seen on the next page.

If we recall, Standard Work is the foundation of our Management System. We build the remaining components, i.e., Sensory Management, Self-Accountability, Self-Discipline, Coaching and Development, upon our Standard Work. Only with Standard Work can we create a Sacred Workday culture.

Once we complete this workshop, the process manager (the learner) should share the value stream Target Condition with the frontline employees and work on creating a short-term, process-level

Target Condition two weeks out.

| Day 1 | Day 2 | Day 3 | Day 4 | Day 5 |
|---|---|---|---|---|
| ❑ Create Standard Work ❑ Create Sensory Management | ❑ Create Self-Accountability ❑ Create Self-Discipline (Leader Standard Work) | ❑ Create Development Plan | ❑ Initiate Catch-Ball process ❑ Vision ❑ Enterprise Future State Value Stream Map ❑ Future State Value Stream Map ❑ Standard Work | ❑ Continue Catch-Ball process ❑ Development Plans ❑ Ready to begin PDCA |

Figure 5.10 - Five-day workshop to determine the process-level Management System.

However, before exploring how we will do so, let's take a quick look at the structure for additional five-day workshops we will use to create our second and third value stream Target Conditions.

## Production System (Looking Ahead)

| Day 1 | Day 2 | Day 3 | Day 4 | Day 5 |
|---|---|---|---|---|
| ❑ Kickoff ❑ Review Future State Value Stream Map ❑ Understand current state of processes we want to create flow between | ❑ Create new Job Instruction Breakdown for cross-train and/or synchronize | ❑ Create cell design with co-location and limited WIP | ❑ Create specs for autonomation | ❑ Redesign work space ❑ Begin to train |

Figure 5.11 - Five-day workshop to create the second process-level Target Condition that achieves flow.

It is important to note that in the second Target Condition we begin to look at information technology (IT) production changes. With stable processes in place, we will be in a much better position to autonomate. Too often, businesses automate a broken process and spend a lot of money in doing so.

| Day 1 | Day 2 | Day 3 |
|---|---|---|
| ❏ Kickoff<br>❏ Review Future State Value Stream Map<br>❏ Review Current State Value Stream Map<br>❏ Create new schedule that levels load and mix | ❏ Design pull system<br>❏ Redesign work space | ❏ Begin to train |

**Figure 5.12** - Three-day workshop to create the third process-level Target Condition that achieves pulls, and levels the load and mix.

Remember, after we set each Target Condition – an update to our Production System – it is essential we update our Management System to ensure the two systems are in sync. Both should continuously be updated as we continually improve.

Now let's look at how to set short-term, process-level Target Conditions.

## 2-Week PDCA

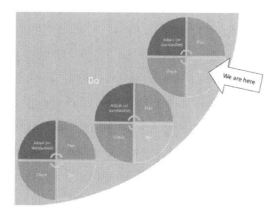

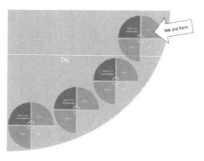

**Figure 5.13** - Four 2-week PDCA cycles at the process level, embedded into the more long 2-month PDCA cycle at the value stream level.

In a 2-month time frame, we will have four opportunities to set 2-week Target Conditions. We don't want to waste any of them!

We have done the hard work to expand the value stream-level Target Condition with more detail at the process level. Setting even shorter-term, process-level Target Conditions are more about giving teams autonomy on how fast to navigate through the knowledge threshold. This exercise should not take long: a matter of looking at the 2-month Target Condition and deciding how far along they want to be in 2 weeks. Again, depending on what they choose, the

Management System should be updated.

## DAILY / INTRA-DAILY PDCA

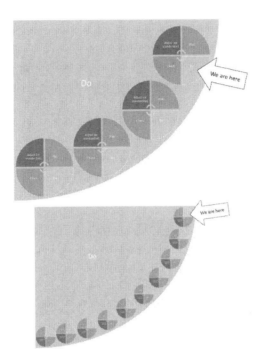

**Figure 5.14** - Ten daily PDCA cycles at the frontline/process level, embedded into the more ambitious 2-week PDCA cycles.

Up until now, we have been preparing for the "big game." Each day we wake for work, we should feel confident knowing that we have a well-thought-out plan grounded in strong principles and proven unifying rituals that allow us to *embrace problems and transform them into continuous improvement, thus, restoring employee freshness and strength.*

Let's walk through those unifying rituals.

At a high level, each day should comprise of:

1. Reviewing a plan to start the day
2. Doing the work
3. Making small adjustments
4. Reflecting on how we did to plan at the end of the day

We see another view on the next page that gives more detail on the intra-daily rituals.

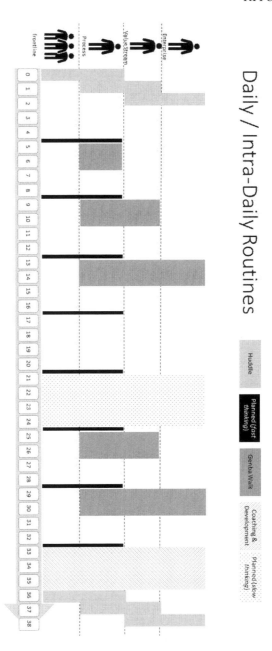

5.15 - A view of the unifying rituals performed in our business on any given day.

## Reviewing a Plan to Start the Day

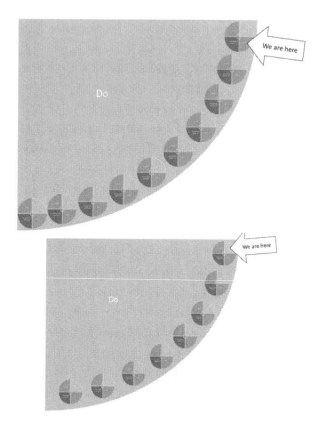

**Figure 5.16** - Eight hourly PDCA cycles embedded into each day.

One of the biggest differentiators between those who achieve a Sacred Workday and those who remain profane is how they start their day. Those who achieve a Sacred Workday wake up early and with a plan. Their ikigai motivates them. They are alive! Those who remain profane wake up late, rushed, and without a plan.

There is a Buddhist story told by Zen Master, Thich Nhat Hanh, in which he describes a man on a horse. When asked where he was going he replies, *I don't know. The horse is taking me.*[33] For most people, this is the case: their day is a horse taking them wherever it pleases. Not us!

## Process Level

For us, a Sacred Workday begins by creating alignment around what success looks like for the day and what our plan is to achieve it (why). This coordination happens by the process manager leading the frontline team (who) through the Planning Huddle (what) using an agenda (how). This meeting takes place at the Demand and Capacity and Performance Boards (where) to have a focused discussion that is brief, yet powerful. To make the Huddle useful, it must start before production (when), which requires the process manager and frontline staff to arrive before the start of their shift.

For example, if a shift starts at 8 am, and we schedule the Planning Huddle for 15 minutes, employees should arrive at 7:40 to settle in and get ready for the Huddle. As a consultant, I have met resistance to this. Upon reflection, I realize that when I did, it was a direct result of not explaining the *why*. If we recall the intro, our why is to make the 8 hours we spend at work sacred so that we can become a better person for our customers, the people we care for, and, ultimately, ourselves. If we can do so by arriving to work 20 minutes before our shift, there should be no resistance.

Each process within the value stream should begin the day with the same unifying ritual which happens simultaneously.

## Value Stream Level

Immediately following the Planning Huddles, the process managers are responsible for checking up on the start of production. Upon completing that task (when), they should attend the value stream Planning Huddle which follows a similar format to the process Planning Huddle. At the value stream level, the value stream manager leads the process managers (who) through the Planning Huddle (what) using an agenda (how). This meeting takes place at the Demand and Capacity and Performance Boards (where). However, in addition to discussing what success looks like for the value stream and the plan to get there, escalations from the process level are addressed (why). At the value stream level, if one process needs capacity and another process has additional capacity and an employee who is cross-trained to do the work, we can shift resources as a counter-measure. It important to note that this Huddle is also a very efficient way for the value stream manager to receive information; specifically:

- How do my managers define success for the day (and does it tie back to success of the value stream)?
- Do my managers have a plan to achieve success?
- What do my managers need from me as a leader to help them achieve success?

This 15-minute Huddle replaces the need for profane meetings in conference rooms that typically do not have an agenda and waste everyone's sacred time.

## Enterprise Level

Immediately following the value stream Huddles, there should be an enterprise-level Huddle which follows the same logic as the previous Huddles, but with an enterprise lens. In other words, we can now level capacity across various value streams.

At the beginning of our Sacred Workday journey, although the value streams we target will be Market and Sell, Recruit, Hire, and Onboard, Train, and focus value stream, we should still invite the other value stream leaders as it is vital to keep them engaged as they will be next.

## Deliver Value

Now that we know what we need to do and what the plan is to do it, it is time to do it! We also know that we have the employees who are adequately skilled in executing (using Job Instruction). However, we cannot control external factors, and problems will always arise. We embrace them!

## Unplanned (fast thinking)

Throughout the day, at any point in time, the Andon can and should be triggered. It is critical that employees feel comfortable enough to trigger the Andon any time they cannot perform the Standard Work. Once employees do this, a process manager should follow our Standard Work for problem-solving as depicted in the image on the next page.

As you can see, when the Andon is triggered, employees will use type 1 thinking, i.e., the reptilian brain. However, they will have a unifying ritual using the Coaching Kata questions to guide them. At this point, they are looking to put a short-term counter-measure (I tend to shy away from the word *solution* as it implies the problem will never occur again) in place to ensure the delivery of value to the customer is uninterrupted. The problem should be recorded using Pareto analysis to allow for more in-depth reflection through use of type 2 thinking later where we will seek to get to the root-cause and put in place stronger counter-measures. As we mature in our Sacred Workday culture, employees will find it easier to get to the actual root-cause and implement stronger countermeasures when using type 1 thinking. In the beginning of our journey, this will be very difficult to do.

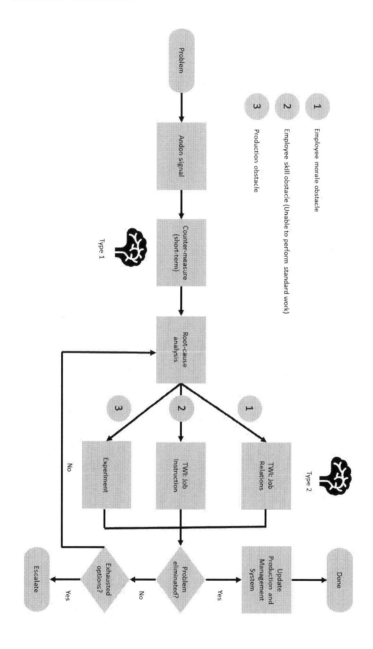

**Figure 5.17** - In this diagram, we see our end-to-end Standard Work for problem-solving.

*Planned (fast thinking)*

In addition to Unplanned (fast thinking), we will also have dedicated time at every pitch to check and adjust through Planned (fast thinking). One of the primary reasons for initiating Planned (fast thinking) at each pitch is to ensure the Management System is working as designed to develop trust with our frontline staff.

When the Management System is initially rolled out, employees will not trigger the Andon. This lack of participation is to be expected. Whether we realized it or not, we have come to accept problems as the norm habitually or to hide them in fear. Making a paradigm shift is essential. When managers visit the genba at each pitch, it is their opportunity to build trust and to reinforce the *unifying rituals that embrace problems and transform them into continuous improvement, thus, restoring employee freshness and strength.*

At each pitch, the process manager should visit the Sensory Management at the genba and engage with frontline employees. They should follow the routine Coaching Kata questions highlighted in chapter 4:

- What is the Target Condition? (for the last pitch)
- What is our Actual Condition?
    - What countermeasures did we put in place?
    - What did we expect to happen?
    - What happened?
    - What did we learn?
- What problems are in our way?
- What countermeasure do we need to put in place?
    - Who will be self-accountable?
    - What do we expect to happen?
- By when will it be put in place? (again, this is redundant as it should be put in place immediately)

The order in which a manager asks these questions matter. Each question builds off the previous question. As a result, at any point in time, if the frontline employees are unable to answer a question, the process manager knows where to focus the next step.

For example, if the Sensory Management is not up-to-date and the frontline cannot answer how they are performing relative to the Standard Work, the process manager should seek to understand what problems are impeding them from updating the Sensory Management. They should then determine the next step and see if leadership can help in any way. Once performance to the Standard Work is understood, we can shift the conversation to capturing problems related to the process and working on putting countermeasures in place.

## Direct Observation

It is critical that the process manager make time to go to the genba for direct observation of the work. At any point in time, if the frontline employee cannot demonstrate the ability to perform the Standard Work due to lack of skill, the process manager should take the time to use Job Instruction to retrain them. Direct observation is also critical to ensure employees are correctly triggering the Andon light when they cannot follow the Standard Work.

It is imperative that value stream managers and executives also visit the genba to ensure the Management System is working as designed and to build trust. If the value stream manager and executives do not implement this Self-Discipline, the Management System will quickly crumble.

## Planned (slow thinking)

At some point in the day, it is also critical to have time set aside for Planned (slow thinking). I find it's helpful to have all process teams schedule this at the same time daily. If they are dealing with problems at the process level, a value stream manager or executive can optionally attend. If there is a problem that spans across several processes (at the value stream level), then the value stream manager should attend to ensure our ritual is consistent with the Shingo principle of *think systemically*. The value stream manager should protect the time as part of their Leader Standard Work whether they are needed or not. If they are not required, they can use the time for other work, i.e., Self-Accountability, etc.

I would recommend spending 1-hour a day on Planned (slow thinking), although this can vary depending on the need. If more significant problems persist, sometimes it is necessary to extend this to full or multi-day sessions. However, if the 1-hour a day is not needed, the team should question whether their current Target Condition is beyond their collective knowledge threshold. A Target Condition is intended to create problems so that we can embrace them and transform them into continuous improvement.

During the 1-hour, it is crucial to conduct root-cause analysis, deploying 5-why thinking and going to the genba when needed. Once we correctly understand the root-cause of any problem, we will find that obstacles fall into three buckets as seen on the image on page 184:

1) Will-problems
2) Skill problems
3) Production problems

## Will Problems

Will-problems can arise for various reasons. Luckily for us, Training Within Industry has also developed a structured approach to dealing with these issues called *Job Relations* or *JR*. TWI defines JR as:

> *Job Relations teaches the foundations of positive employee relations. Developing and maintaining these good relationships prevents problems from arising and is paramount to earn loyalty and cooperation from others.*

Whenever will-problems occur, a manager should deploy JR.

## Skill Problems

Whenever skill problems arise, meaning the employee is incapable of performing the Standard Work, the process manager should deploy Job Instruction as a countermeasure. If we recall, *if the learner hasn't learned, the teacher hasn't taught*. Thus, rather than blame the employee, the process manager should question whether he deployed JI correctly. This problem is an opportunity for the process manager to reflect and remedy the situation.

## Production Problems

Lastly, there are production problems that will keep our frontline employees from executing the Standard Work. These are typically problems related to quality issues with the inputs received, tools not working correctly, unevenness of work (mura), or portions of the process that are too difficult for our employees to repeatedly execute without the help of Job-Aids or Autonomation (muri).

In all the scenarios above, we should formulate experiments and implement countermeasures to mitigate these problems. Whenever a countermeasure yields an improvement, we should update both our Production System and Management System. If countermeasures are exhausted, and they still do not mitigate the problem, then-and-only-then, escalation should occur.

Once a Target Condition is met (that isn't the 2-month Target Condition), the team should use Planned (slow thinking) time to select the next Target Condition.

## Error-Proofing and the Role of IT

Every problem is an opportunity to make the work easier for employees. Every time a problem occurs, employees should ask the question, *what would the requirements be, i.e., the logic, for Autonomation that would prevent this problem from ever happening again?*

At one of my clients, the same problem kept on happening

repeatedly. When an insurance company requested a second opinion on a physician review, our dispatchers would select the initial reviewer by mistake. The reviewer, rather than notify us, reviewed the case again to receive payment. Initially, we updated our Job Instruction Breakdown and trained our employees to double-check. However, when production was stressful, they would forget. As a result, we worked with our IT team to develop simple logic to remove previous reviewers from the drop-down list in the system, eliminating the burden from our frontline employees. The problem never happened again.

Although this example is underwhelming, there is a valuable lesson here. IT groups are often consumed developing large-scale changes. Rather than do so, they should dedicate capacity to smaller changes that can be implemented quickly based on input from frontline employees. When done, frontline employees begin to witness IT work for them. As such, more and more problems with technology will emerge that previously were accepted. We may even see that the large-scale changes – that often cost a lot of money – are unnecessary.

## Reflect: Check and Adjust

At the end of the shift, there should be a Reflection Huddle where the team can check and adjust for the next shift. This time for reflection is critical, also allowing the team to celebrate and recognize accomplishments.

I find that most people go through the profane workday just doing tasks; rarely reflecting on whether on how they performed those tasks or on whether those tasks even added value.

Unlike the Planning Huddle, frontline employees should not be expected to stay late; thus, we should plan for the last 15 minutes of an employee's shift to be non-production time (our takt calculation should account for this). If there is a need for overtime, the team can discuss that at this Huddle.

Like the Planning Huddle at the beginning of the shift, upon the process level completing their Reflection Huddle, there will be a value stream and enterprise reflection to complete the cycle and ensure our rituals are in alignment with the Shingo principle of *constancy of purpose*.

At the end of the last ritual for the day, everyone should go home feeling proud that they delivered value to our customers as promised. At a minimum, everyone should have learned how to improve the way we do so via *performing unifying rituals that embrace problems and transform them into continuous improvement, thus, restoring employee freshness and strength*. With each day, we see the boring, mundane workday turn into a Sacred Workday and we realize our purpose.

# 5 | SUMMARY

- Certain unifying rituals are what we use to build our Production System and Management System.
- Once we do, another set of unifying rituals are used to iterate towards a series of Target Conditions, Challenges, yearly targets, and, ultimately, our Vision.
- There are unifying rituals that occur at different intervals with different focuses:
  - At a yearly interval, the focus is on the enterprise and what we want to achieve for the year.
  - Every six months, the focus is on the value stream and creating a transformation that will allow us to deliver value to our customers faster, better, and cheaper.
  - Every two months, the focus is on achieving Target Conditions that work towards the value stream transformation.
  - Every two weeks, the focus is on achieving short-term Target Conditions that work towards the value stream Target Conditions. These Target Conditions are less intimidating and welcome experimentation and fast failure.
  - Every day, the focus is on taking a step or experimenting towards our short-term Target Condition, *performing unifying rituals that embrace problems and transforming them into continuous improvement, thus, restoring employee freshness and strength.*
- We treat each day as an athletic game:
  - We begin each shift with a Planning Huddle.
  - We have Intermediate Huddles throughout the shift which include:
    - Unplanned (fast thinking)
    - Planned (fast thinking)
    - Planned (slow thinking)

- We end each shift with a Reflection Huddle.
- With each unifying ritual, we achieve a Sacred Workday culture and realize our purpose.

# 5 | EXERCISE

Time for reflection is up! It's time to roll up our sleeves and start to create a Sacred Workday.

- Execute yearly planning session with executives.
- Play Catch-Ball with value stream managers.
- Execute 6-month planning via Value Stream Mapping.
- Play Catch-Ball with process managers.
- Execute 2-month planning for value stream-level Target Conditions.
- Play Catch-Ball with frontline employees.
- Executive 2-week planning for short-term Target Conditions.
- Begin the daily/intra-daily unifying rituals to realize a Sacred Workday.
- Be your purpose!

# 6 | GROWTH

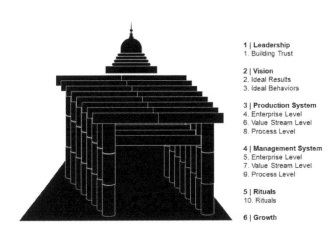

**1 | Leadership**
1. Building Trust

**2 | Vision**
2. Ideal Results
3. Ideal Behaviors

**3 | Production System**
4. Enterprise Level
6. Value Stream Level
8. Process Level

**4 | Management System**
5. Enterprise Level
7. Value Stream Level
9. Process Level

**5 | Rituals**
10. Rituals

**6 | Growth**

As the picture suggests, growth is about repeating what we did on a small scale at a larger one. There are 10,000 torii that lead to the Fushimi Inari Shrine. For us, each torii represents a transformation of a new value stream, a new process, and, ultimately, all the new employees who begin to practice the unifying rituals.

Up until now, we have transformed one focus value stream and its' supporting value streams. We can't stop there. The temple comes when and only when our entire business has been transformed, creating a Sacred Workday culture where we *perform unifying rituals that embrace problems and transform them into continuous improvement, thus, restoring employee freshness and strength.* We cannot have the profane and sacred co-exist. We must either be profane or sacred or run the risk of being like the Church of Laodicea:

*I know your deeds, that you are neither cold nor hot. I wish you were either one or the other! So, because you are lukewarm--neither hot nor cold--I am about to spit you out of my mouth.*[34]

However, if we follow the formula in this book without taking shortcuts, we will achieve our purpose:

- To make the 8 hours we spend at work sacred so that we can become better people for our customers, the people we care for, and, ultimately, ourselves;
- To share the rewards (financial and non-financial) that a Sacred Workday generates with our employees and customers; and
- To provide a job for life to all those who will want to participate in creating a Sacred Workday.

As we grow, the difficulty will be in maintaining the Self-Discipline required to make a Sacred Workday a reality. There will be temptations along the way: to skip a Huddle here and there, to not go to the genba, to focus on the ideal results with no regard to the ideal behaviors, to work in comfortable silos, to hide waste and avoid the difficult conversations, to not take the time to coach and develop each other... We will resist! Too much is at stake if we genuinely believe in our purpose. It won't be easy, but when we achieve it (and we will achieve it), we will never look back!

# 6 | SUMMARY

- Growth is about repeating what we did with one focus value stream and its' supporting value streams to our entire business.
- To grow, we must remain disciplined.
- Along the way, there will be many temptations.
- We will avoid them all and achieve a Sacred Workday and never look back!

# 6 | EXERCISE

- Identify your next value stream and repeat the process outlined in this book.
- Avoid temptations and continue to maintain the Self-Discipline.
- Never look back!

# REFERENCES

## NOTE FROM AUTHOR

1. McKay, B., & McKay, K. (2013, December 19). The Power of Ritual: The Creation of Sacred Time and Space in a Profane World. Retrieved from The Art of Manliness: https://www.artofmanliness.com/2013/12/19/the-power-of-ritual-the-creation-of-sacred-time-and-space-in-a-profane-world/

2. Morris, D. Z. (2017, September 1). U.S. Job Satisfaction Hits Its Highest Level Since 2005. Retrieved from Fortune: http://fortune.com/2017/09/01/job-satisfaction-highest-since-2005/

3. Sinek, S. (2009, September). How Great Leaders Inspire Action. Retrieved from TED: https://www.ted.com/talks/simon_sinek_how_great_leaders_inspire_action

## INTRODUCTION

4. Gyatso, G. K. (2002). Understanding the Mind: The Nature and Power of the Mind.

5. Gyatso, G. K. (2017). Transform Your Life: A Blissful Journey.

6. Sentis. (2012, November 6). Neuroplasticity. Retrieved from YouTube: https://www.youtube.com/watch?v=ELpfYCZa87g

7. Lean Enterprise Institute. (n.d.). What is Lean? Retrieved from Lean Enterprise Institute: https://www.Lean.org/WhatsLean/

8.  Custers, E. (2017, August 6). Reflex Action and Reflex Arc: What Happens When You Accidentally Touch a Hot Pot. Retrieved from Owlcation: https://owlcation.com/stem/Here-is-what-happens-when-you-accidentally-touch-a-hot-pot

9.  The Shingo Institute. (n.d.). Retrieved from Shino Prize: http://www.shingoprize.org/model

10. Wright, R. (2017). Why Buddhism is True: The Science and Philosophy of Meditation and Enlightenment.

## 1 | LEADERSHIP

11. Darabont, F. (Director). (1994). The Shawshank Redemption [Motion Picture].

12. Schein, E. H. (2013). Humble Inquiry: The Gentle Art of Asking Instead of Telling.

## 2 | VISION

13. Merriam-Webster. (2018, February 19). Merriam-. Retrieved from Merriam-Webster: https://www.merriam-webster.com/dictionary/visionary

14. Garcia, H., & Miralles, F. (2016). Ikigai: The Japenese Secret to a Long and Happy Life.

15. Wikipedia. (n.d.). W. Edwards Deming. Retrieved from Wikipedia: https://en.wikipedia.org/wiki/W._Edwards_Deming

16. Sinek, S. (2018, February 26). Retrieved from BrainyQuote.com: https://www.brainyquote.com/quotes/simon_sinek_568142

## 3 | PRODUCTION SYSTEM

17. Rother, M., & Shook, J. (1999). Learning to See: Value Stream Mapping to Add Value and Eliminate MUDA 1st Edition.

18. Wikipedia. (n.d.). Autonomation. Retrieved from Wikipedia: https://en.wikipedia.org/wiki/Autonomation

19. Rother, M. (2009). Toyota Kata: Managing People for Improvement, Adaptiveness and Superior Results 1st Edition.

20. Training Within Industry Institute. (n.d.). History. Retrieved from Training Within Industry Institute: http://www.twi-institute.org/training-within-industry/history/

21. Graupp, P. & Wrona, R. (2015). The TWI Workbook: Essential Skills for Supervisors, Second Edition 2nd Edition

22. Wikipedia. (n.d.). Manufacturing supermarket. Retrieved from Wikipedia: https://en.wikipedia.org/wiki/Manufacturing_supermarket

## 4 | MANAGEMENT SYSTEM

23. Mann, D. (2014). Creating a Lean Culture: Tools to Sustain Lean Conversions, Third Edition.

24. Willink, J. (2017). Discipline Equals Freedom: Field Manual.

25. Wikipedia. (n.d.). Kinesthetic learning.
https://en.wikipedia.org/wiki/Kinesthetic_learning

26.  Okrent, A. (2014, February 2). The true origin story of the football Huddle. Retrieved from The Week:
http://theweek.com/articles/451763/true-origin-story-football-Huddle

27. Kahneman, D. (2011). Thinking, Fast and Slow.

28. Wikipedia. (n.d.). Wikipedia. Retrieved from Andon (manufacturing):
https://en.wikipedia.org/wiki/Andon_(manufacturing)

29. Csikszentmihalyi, M. (2008). Flow: The Psychology of Optimal Experience.

30. Wikipedia. (n.d.). GROW model. Retrieved from Wikipedia:
https://en.wikipedia.org/wiki/GROW_model

31. Stone, D. a. (2014). Thanks for the Feedback: The Science and Art of Receiving Feedback Well.

32. Patten, E. (2016, July 1). Pew Research. Retrieved from Racial, gender wage gaps persist in U.S. despite some progress:
http://www.pewresearch.org/fact-tank/2016/07/01/racial-gender-wage-gaps-persist-in-u-s-despite-some-progress/

## 5 | RITUALS

33. Hanh, T. N. (1997). The Heart of the Buddha's Teaching.

# 6 | GROWTH

34. The Bible: The New International Version. (n.d.). Revelation 3:15-16.

# ACKNOWLEDGEMENTS

Sacred Workday was made possible by those who entrusted me to guide them. These entrepreneurs put the well-being of their businesses in my hands. They paid me to make mistakes and sharpen my craft. If it were not for them, this book would not be. I would like to especially recognize two of these individuals who allowed me to change their companies at the principle-level and create a Sacred Workday.

Thank you Andrew Rowe, CEO of AllMed Healthcare Management. It was there that I refined my skills at building a Production System, Management System, and rituals.

Thank you Dr. Oleg Maksimov, CEO and owner of Columbia Pain and Spine Institute. It was there that I refined my skills at using Humble Inquiry to build trust.

# ABOUT THE TYPE

This book was set in Sabon, a typeface designed by the well-known German typographer Jan Tschichold (1902-74). Sabon's design is based upon the original letterforms of sixteenth-century French type designer Claude Garamond and was created specifically to be used for three sources: foundry type for hand composition, Linotype, and Monotype. Tschichold named his typeface for the famous Frankfurt typefounder Jacques Sabon (c. 1520-80).

# PROCEEDS

Your purchase of this book has contributed $1 to
Operation Warrior Wellness.

For more information, please visit

https://www.davidlynchfoundation.org/veterans.html

# ABOUT THE AUTHOR

In 2017, Daniel became the first and only Lean Gold Certified professional in non-manufacturing (one of eight total) as recognized by the Shingo Institute, SME, and AME (the gold standard for Lean certification). To receive it, Daniel had to demonstrate mastery of his craft by transforming several organizations at the enterprise level, from the C-suite to the frontlines.

That same year, Daniel began Gold Sensei to introduce clients to a purer version of Lean that aligned more closely with the core principles presented by Taiichi Ohno. In his experience, he had to clean up behind too many consultants who solely introduce clients to Lean tools without teaching the principles.

www.thegoldsensei.com
www.sacredworkday.com
Twitter: @thegoldsensei

Made in the USA
Columbia, SC
01 February 2021